THE COMMON PURSUIT

Simon Gray's new play follows the lives of six friends from their meeting in the sixties when they first come together as Cambridge undergraduates, through the following twenty years to the onset of middle age. Although on the surface a comedy of literary manners, *The Common Pursuit* is also a study of love and friendship, deceit and compromise.

Published to coincide with its premiere, *The Common Pursuit* opened at the Lyric Theatre, Hammersmith, in a production directed by Harold Pinter, in summer 1984.

The photograph of Simon Gray on the back cover is reproduced by courtesy of the Sunday Telegraph.

by the same author

Plays

Sleeping Dog (published by Faber)
Wise Child (published by Faber)
Dutch Uncle (published by Faber)
Spoiled (published by Eyre Methuen)
The Idiot (published by Eyre Methuen)
Butley (published by Eyre Methuen)
Otherwise Engaged, Two Sundays *and* Plaintiffs and Defendants
    (published by Eyre Methuen)
Dog Days (published by Eyre Methuen)
The Rear Column, Molly *and* Man in a Side-Car (published by
    Eyre Methuen)
Close of Play *and* Pig in a Poke (published by Eyre Methuen)
Stage Struck (published by Eyre Methuen)
Quartermaine's Terms (published by Methuen London)

Novels

Colmain (published by Faber)
Little Portia (published by Faber)
Simple People (published by Faber)
A Comeback for Stark (under the pseudonym Hamish Reade,
    published by Faber)

Translation

Tartuffe *by Molière*

Simon Gray

THE COMMON PURSUIT

Scenes from the Literary Life

METHUEN · LONDON AND NEW YORK

A METHUEN PAPERBACK

First published in Great Britain as a Methuen Paperback original
by Methuen London Ltd, 11 New Fetter Lane, London EC4P 4EE,
and in the United States of America by Methuen Inc, 733 Third
Avenue, New York NY 10017.
Copyright © 1984 by Simon Gray
Set in IBM 10pt. Journal by 𝍄 Tek-Art, Croydon, Surrey
Printed in Great Britain by Whitstable Litho Ltd
Whitstable, Kent

British Library Cataloguing in Publication Data

Gray, Simon
  The common pursuit. — (Methuen modern plays)
  I. Title
  822' .914   PR6057.R33

ISBN 0-413-55990-4

CAUTION

For Ben and Lucy

Characters

STUART
MARIGOLD
MARTIN
NICK
PETER
HUMPHRY

ACT ONE

Scene One

STUART's *rooms, in Cambridge. Twenty years ago. It is mid-morning.*

There is the door (and an oak door behind it) stage left. Stage right, a window and window seat. A door, centre, closed, to the bedroom.

There is a table in the middle, covered with typescripts, books, etc.

There is a sofa, two arm-chairs, a chair for the table. Books etc, on shelves (rather haphazardly) around the walls.

There is a gramophone, stage left. A record is playing on it.

STUART *and* MARIGOLD *are sitting on the window seat, in the sunlight, holding hands, staring at each other intently.*

MARIGOLD *strokes* STUART's *cheek. They kiss, gently, on the lips. The kiss becomes more passionate. They stand, kissing.*

MARIGOLD. Oh you — oh you! (*They kiss again.*) Come on — come on! (*Pulling him, laughingly, towards the bedroom door.*)

STUART (*resisting*). No, we can't. They'll be here any minute.

MARIGOLD. We'll be extremely quick. Like lightning.

STUART. But I don't want to be extremely quick, like lightning. I want to be extremely slow. Forever, in fact.

MARIGOLD (*after a small pause*). Forever?

STUART (*after a little pause*). Absolutely. Forever.

MARIGOLD. And afterwards will you write a poem about it?

STUART. No, it wouldn't be good enough. But you can. And I'll publish it. How's that? Or I can publish your last letter. Instead of the usual manifesto. In fact, your letter can be our manifesto. (*Laughing*.)

MARIGOLD. It would be your only issue. We'd both be sent down on the strength of the ps alone. One of my bolder strokes, I thought.

STUART. Yes, you're frankly disgusting. (*He glances at his watch, looks out of the window*.) Oh here comes one of them now, what's his name — um, Martin — Martin — oh hell, I told you Martin — the one with the loot and the zeal for service.

MARIGOLD (*staring out of the window*). Isn't that our greatest living poet figure?

STUART. What?

MARIGOLD. Hubert Parkin. The man you claim is the greatest living —

STUART. Christ, it is! He must have come up for the big dinner last night — where's he going? (*He peers*.) Into one of the guest rooms. Come on. (*To* MARIGOLD.)

MARIGOLD. Where?

STUART. To see him, of course. Tell him about the magazine. Ask him if he'll contribute. Well, why not? He might. Anyway, let's try. At least I'll have met him. Come on.

They cross, STUART *flings the door open.*

MARTIN *enters.*

STUART. Oh hello, this is — um, look, there's somebody we've got to see, we won't be a minute, make yourself at home. And tell anyone else we'll be right back.

MARTIN. Oh right.

STUART (*gestures*). Change the record, if you want. (*He goes off with* MARIGOLD.)

MARTIN *stands uncertainly. He crosses to the gramophone, around which is a litter of record sleeves. He picks up one. It is empty. He reads the title of the work, nods, puts the record down. He wanders over to the table, glances at the typescripts, etc; sees a letter, glances quickly around, then picks up the letter, begins to read it, very quickly. He is clearly amazed by the contents. He puts the letter down, in exactly the same position, adjusting it slightly, and moves away from the table to the window seat. Looks out of the window, sees somebody he recognises, and sits down on the window seat. Assumes a deeply listening posture.*

HUMPHRY appears at the door. MARTIN is enacting too absorbed to be aware of him.

HUMPHRY (*entering properly*). Stuart not here then?

MARTIN (*starting*). Oh. No, they've just dashed off somewhere. But they'll be back in a minute. He said to wait.

HUMPHRY sits down. There is a pause.

Marvellous stuff, isn't it?

HUMPHRY *grunts.*

Do you like Vivaldi?

HUMPHRY. Yes. But I like Bach more. Which this is.

MARTIN. Really? Are you sure?

HUMPHRY. Yes.

MARTIN. Oh. Well, you're probably right. I had some idea it was that Vivaldi piece in E major — which Bach is it then, do you know?

HUMPHRY. No.

The record comes to an end. There is a clicking and whirring from the gramophone.

HUMPHRY gets up, goes over to it. He deftly stops the gramophone, removes the record and looks around for the sleeve. He picks up the sleeve MARTIN had looked at.

MARTIN. What was it precisely?

HUMPHRY (*puts down the sleeve and glances at the record*). The suite in A.

MARTIN. Vivaldi, you mean?

HUMPHRY. No, Bach of course. (*He picks up another sleeve, which is empty, checks the record against it and slips it in.*)

MARTIN. Really! You must have a terrific feeling for passages of music. I only know them when I've heard them hundreds of times before. And then I get them wrong. (*He laughs.*)

HUMPHRY *sits down.*

You're Humphry Taylor, aren't you?

HUMPHRY. That's right.

MARTIN. And you're doing history, isn't it?

HUMPHRY. Moral Sciences.

MARTIN. Oh. Well, I'm Martin Musgrove. I'm in English. I suppose you've come about the magazine too? Have you written something for it?

HUMPHRY. I sent in some poems. What about you? Have you written anything?

MARTIN. Oh no — well, actually I did submit a little thing I'd written. A sort of prose poem about well, cats, actually. (*He laughs.*) But Stuart sent it back saying I had far more grasp of cats than I did of prose or poetry, so I'd better stick to those. Quite right. It was pretty embarrassing, when I read it through. I haven't got any talent at all, you see. But I'm interested in publishing, so I want to work on the magazine from that point of view. The business side, you know, helping with subscriptions, advertising, anything of that sort. Is he going to publish your poems?

HUMPHRY. No. I've come to get them back.

MARTIN. Oh. What didn't he like about them?

HUMPHRY. He liked them. It's me. I don't like them.

MARTIN. Really, why not?

HUMPHRY. Because they make me feel sick. In fact, I've decided to give up writing. Poems, anyway.

MARTIN. But mightn't you eventually write some that don't make you feel sick.

HUMPHRY. Possibly. But it's not worth the risk. Besides I'm going to be a professional philosopher. So I'll have to concentrate on thinking until I've got my First and a job in a university.

MARTIN. That's what you want, is it?

HUMPHRY. I haven't any choice. As you can't be a professional philosopher except in a university.

MARTIN. Do you want to be in any particular university?

HUMPHRY. This one will do.

MARTIN (*laughs slightly*). Any particular college?

HUMPHRY. This one will do.

MARTIN. Well — that's quite a prediction, really.

HUMPHRY. It wasn't meant to be. More like an obituary, in fact. But if I'm going to institutionalise myself, I suppose I might as well do it in one of the better institutions.

MARTIN. I wish I had that sort of confidence about my own future. I only thought of publishing because I can't think of anything else.

NICK (*enters, coughing slightly, looks around*). Where's Stuart then?

MARTIN. He said to wait, they'd be right back.

NICK. They — oh, of course, Marigold. Well, isn't there any coffee on the go or anything? I've got a hangover.

MARTIN. Really? How did you get it?

NICK. Drank too much. In fact, look, what's that stuff, slimey, thick and yellow?

HUMPHRY. That covers a large number of revolting substances.

MARTIN. Oh, it must be avocaat, mustn't it? You know. Egg Nog.

NICK. That explains it. I'm allergic to eggs. Probably allergic to nogs too. If they're what they sound like. It was that bloody girl from Girton — Muriel what's-it?

MARTIN. Hoftstadt?

NICK. Yes, she produced it. I was perfectly all right until then.

Coasting along on white wine, martini, rum, scotch, that sort of thing. But then that's Muriel, always there when you least want her, passing out egg nogs when you least want them, she should have been a nurse. (*He laughs and coughs slightly*.)

MARTIN. Did Muriel give the party?

NICK. Do you think I'd go to a party given by Muriel Hoftstadt? No, no, it was some prick, prickette from King's, secretary of their literary society, Jeremy — Jeremy —

MARTIN. Astle.

NICK. To meet that woman who's written a novel about her menstrual cycle, *Murdering*.

MARTIN. *Mothering*, isn't it?

NICK. What?

MARTIN. Isn't it *Mothering*, not *Murdering*?

NICK. I thought they were synonyms.

MARTIN (*laughs*). Angela Thark.

NICK. What?

MARTIN. That's her name. The novelist's, isn't it? Angela Thark. I wish I'd met her. I got the novel just yesterday, I haven't read it yet. What's she like?

NICK. Much sexier than her prose. Bit of a knock-out really. If you like long legs, big breasts, that sort of thing. I do. But I'm not very selective yet. I'm still a virgin. What about you two? Actually, this room reeks of passion. What were you up to before I came in? (*Laughs, coughs slightly and meets HUMPHRY's eye*.) Don't worry, it wouldn't show, not if Stuart and Marigold have been at it.

MARTIN. Did she have anything interesting to say?

NICK. Who?

MARTIN. Angela Thark? Did she talk about novel writing, that sort of thing?

NICK. Look, could you hold on the incisive questions, just for a moment? I'm about to do something exceptionally difficult.

(*He takes out a cigarette, lights it and inhales.*) Oh God! Yes, here they come, the little buggers, bobbing from iris to pupil and back again. Now the ripples of giddiness — turning into tidal bloody waves of nausea. (*He groans.*)

MARTIN. Is it always like this when you smoke a cigarette?

NICK. Only the first.

HUMPHRY. Why have it then?

NICK. So I can get on to my next. By the third or fourth I won't even notice I'm smoking.

MARTIN. But if the first few are so ghastly, and you don't even notice the rest of them, why don't you just give up?

NICK. What for?

MARTIN. Well — I mean, for one thing you might live longer.

NICK. Oh, you don't live longer, it just seems longer. As Sam Goldwyn said. One of the poets, anyway. (*He wanders shakily to the table, picks up the typescripts, etc.*)

MARTIN. You know, sometimes I think I'm missing out on addiction. I've never been addicted to anything in my life. Not even when I was a child. I mean, I'm normal all the time, which is very boring. For everyone else as well as me. While for you I suppose normal's something you accelerate away from with drinks and cigarettes — (*He stops, aware that* HUMPHRY *is watching* NICK, *who is reading something he has extracted from an envelope.*)

NICK. Boys on their river banks, naked in the sad and dewy dawn. (*He laughs and coughs slightly.*) God, I hate queer literature. (*He reads again.*) Not for publication, at least at this stage, but glad to hear of new magazine, hope it will be noted for its critical vigour — vigour? — rigour, James Harrop, New College, Oxford, oh that explains it, probably not even queer, just Oxford, I knew a Harrop, at prep school, wonder if it's the same one, he was a creep too.

HUMPHRY. You shouldn't do that.

NICK. What? (*He picks up the letter* MARTIN *read earlier and begins to read it.*)

(*He whistles.*) I say, Marigold can really turn it on. A little too well-written for my taste, though. But I suppose that's the problem with having an affair with a literary editor, keeping one's prose up to snuff.

HUMPHRY. I said don't do that.

NICK. Do what?

MARTIN. Yes, well — I must say I've never seen anyone read anyone's private letters, you know.

NICK. Of course you haven't. This is a notable breakthrough. Doing it in public, so to speak. (*He turns a page.*)

HUMPHRY. That's two warnings. You don't get a third. (*He takes a step towards* NICK.)

NICK. Actually it's from the bursar. Inviting him to pay last term's buttery bill.

MARTIN. No, it's not.

NICK (*grins, coughs slightly*). How do you know?

MARTIN. For one thing it's handwritten. And pages long.

NICK. Well, you know the bursar. Anything to make a conquest. Or settle an account.

HUMPHRY (*walks over to him*). Are you going to put it down?

NICK. Are you going to make me?

They stand looking at each other. NICK *tosses the letter on the table.*

It's time I introduced myself. I'm Nick Finchling, special agent. I've adopted this flamboyant personality as a disguise. I'm trying to find ways of persuading Stuart to accept my juvenilia but he says I haven't finished it yet. Actually, I want to do theatre criticism, as I intend to be a big-name theatre reviewer when I grow up, like Ken what's-it, only on the *Sunday Times,* would you really have hit me a moment ago?

HUMPHRY. That moment hasn't passed.

NICK. Will it, if I swear to you that I didn't read a word? You're Humphry Taylor aren't you, the philosopher-poet, I've decided we're going to be friends. It's safer. (*He laughs and coughs.*) Actually Stuart says your poems have genius. And that you're a real find. Who are you — oh, I know, the millionaire orphan, aren't you? (*To* MARTIN.)

MARTIN. Well, I'm not a millionaire.

NICK. But you're quite rich, and if you're an orphan you'll need a friend. (*He laughs.*) I'm your man. Actually I'm the opposite of an orphan, I've got six parents in all, if you include the steps and ex-steps.

PETER (*enters*). Sorry I'm late. Oh. (*Looking around.*)

NICK. Hello Peter. Meet the poet, philosopher and pugilist, Humphrey Taylor, and that chap who wrote the charming little piece about cats that Stuart showed us before returning it to him.

MARTIN. Martin. Martin Musgrove.

NICK. And this is Peter Whetworth. Senior scholar in history, an inevitable First, future Fellow of the college, and consequently one of my closest friends. Stuart says we've to wait for him. Why didn't you come Tharking last night?

PETER (*who has smiled and nodded at* HUMPHRY *and* MARTIN). Oh yes. Sorry. I met up with some people.

NICK. Female people, I suppose.

PETER *laughs.*

More than one female people?

PETER. There were two to begin with, but I whittled them down to one. Actually, I got the wrong one, as the one I whittled turned out to be the one who really wanted me.

NICK. Not Sonia?

PETER. Sonia?

NICK. The nurse at Addenbrooks. You met her in my room last week, when I was rounding up some hopefuls, to lose my virginity with. She wasn't interested in me at all, after you appeared.

PETER. Really? The very pretty one?

NICK. Quite pretty. Quite silly. Terribly nice. And yearns for you. In fact your usual type.

MARTIN. Are you writing for the magazine?

PETER. Not if I can help it. But I'll have some minor function — perhaps I'll be the social officer. Look after the parties, that side of things.

HUMPHRY. I heard your paper. The one you gave to the Maudsley Society.

PETER. Really?

HUMPHRY. It had one or two good things in it. And even some originality.

PETER. Thanks.

NICK. I bet he doesn't say that to all the boys. (*To* PETER.) Tell me about it. Last night. I'm anxious to acquire any information I can on this sex business, all I'm sure of at the moment is that I'm not queer. So what did you do? Did you take her back? Or get her to take you to her place? Or what? How? When? Where? And so on. With illustrations. And I'll invite Sonia back for you, as a reward.

PETER *laughs*.

HUMPHRY. Can we have some music instead. (*Little pause.*) If we're going to wait, could we at least do something worthwhile.

NICK. I advise you not to resist him. He has a powerful personality. (*He goes to the gramophone.*) What would you like to hear?

HUMPHRY. Wagner would probably be the most inappropriate. So let's have him.

NICK. I don't know if Stuart goes in for Wagner. (*Hunting.*) Or anything musical, really. Except for reverie and romance. Ah — here's some. (*He puts the record on the gramophone.*) Mainly snatches from the great tunes, from the look of it. I hope it'll do. (*He sits down.*)

WAGNER *fills the room.* NICK *lights a cigarette and coughs.* HUMPHRY *listens.* MARTIN *assumes a listening posture.* PETER *listens idly, smiling pleasantly.*

They remain in that position as the set revolves off, the music still playing, while STUART's *office revolves on,* STUART *at the desk, for Scene Two.*

Scene Two

STUART's *office in Holborn. Eleven years ago. Late morning. The office is large, and could be handsome. But it is dingy. There is a desk, with a telephone on it. An arm-chair, a sofa, a cupboard. Books and magazines on shelves. Bottles of wine lined up on the shelves, opened and half full, as if left over from a party.*
     STUART *is at his desk, reading a typescript. He looks up, glances at the door, checks his watch, goes resolutely back to reading.*
     The telephone rings.
     STUART's *hand leaps out. He checks it. He lifts the telephone and speaks in a disguised voice. Irish.*

STUART. Hello. Well, yes, I think it is. Hang on while I check. Yes. that's right, the office of the *New Literary Review.* Yes, well I'm the window cleaner, you see, and I'm never sure what's on whatever floor I'm on. Who? Well, I'll have a look, who shall I say is calling, if he's here? Right. No, I'm afraid there's no one here by that name. There doesn't seem to be anyone here at all, in fact. Right. Hang on, I'll just get a pencil. (*He doesn't.*) Ready. Yes. Mappin and Mappin, yes, got that —

MARTIN *enters.*

Compelled to institute legal proceedings unless — what? Oh a cheque, right, by the end of the week. OK. I'll leave it here where he can see it. Not at all. Goodbye. (*He hangs up and stares at the telephone.*) I wish the Post Office would cut me off. They keep threatening to, and I'm three months overdue, after all. But I suppose they're too busy disconnecting old age pensioners and emergency services to get round to deserving cases like me.

MARTIN. Was it the printers again?

STUART. Yes, poor old George this time, with his wheeze and his heart condition. They know perfectly well it's me, I think they're quite grateful I pretend I'm not. Otherwise they'd have to threaten me direct. There's some Nescafé and stale milk, or last month's warm white wine.

MARTIN *takes a bottle of wine out of his pocket and hands it to* STUART, *who takes it and goes to look for a cork-screw.*

MARTIN. No word from Peter yet then?

STUART. No.

MARTIN (*looks at his watch*). Well, I suppose it's still a bit early.

STUART. Only just. (*Beginning to open the bottle.*)

MARTIN. Oh, by the way, who's the girl with the Welsh accent?

STUART. Mmmm? (*Struggling with the cork.*)

MARTIN. Well, I 'phoned you at your flat last night, and got this girl with a Welsh accent. Very nice and talkative, but all she seemed to know about anything was that you'd moved out and that Marigold had had to go away.

STUART. Yes — (*Working the cork.*) she's gone to Cheltenham. To visit her parents. One of them is ill or something.

MARTIN. I thought she only had a father.

STUART. That's right. Then that must be the one that's ill. I didn't get on with her mother either. Especially when she was alive. Ah! (*The cork comes out.*)

MARTIN. But then who was the girl with the Welsh accent?

STUART. Marigold's flatmate.

MARTIN. I thought *you* were her flatmate. (*Slight laugh.*)

STUART. Not for a while. Last week we discovered neither of us could afford my share of the rent. So, Marigold moved in some new teacher from her school, who wants a place to stay while she's looking for a flat of her own. Which means that she's paying my share of the rent. Very nice apparently, if slightly incomprehensible, I didn't know she was Welsh.

MARTIN. But where are you living then?

STUART (*pouring wine*). Oh, here and there. (*He hands MARTIN a glass.*)

MARTIN: Thanks. Here and there?

STUART: Well mainly here. In fact, entirely here.

MARTIN. What do you sleep on?

STUART. There's a sofa. And a sleeping bag in the cupboard.

MARTIN. But why on earth don't you come and stay with me? You can have either of the spare rooms. Or both of them. I can move Samantha into my bedroom. Where she longs to be anyway, and would be, if she didn't make me sneeze.

STUART. Yes, I know. And thanks. But I had an odd feeling. To do with territory. That it would be harder to get me out of here if I made it into my lair. I see myself as a threatened lion. Well, some impressive creature, with teeth and jaws, a tattered tiger. A bankrupt rat.

MARTIN. You know, you're extraordinary.

STUART. Really, why?

MARTIN. Well, for one thing, I couldn't live like this. I'd love to be able to. Like one of the heroes or murderers from Russian novels. But I know I couldn't.

STUART. Oh, it's actually quite simple. All it takes is no money. (*He looks at his watch.*) He's getting on towards being late.

MARTIN. Those meetings go on forever. Until lunch even. You know the Arts Council.

STUART. I do.

MARTIN. Peter'll pull it off. You said yourself a man who can hustle a full Oxford fellowship on Peter's credentials, can hustle anything.

STUART. Yes, but on this occasion he's not hustling for himself, he's hustling for me. Perhaps his heart isn't in it. If he hadn't missed the last meeting he might have got our grant doubled then. And the Hubert Parkin party wouldn't have tipped me into bankruptcy. And I wouldn't have needed the money so desperately now.

MARTIN. Well, of course, that was slightly unfortunate — the Parkin party costing so much —

STUART. No, it was the right thing to do. If I hadn't thrown the party I probably wouldn't have got his six new poems.

MARTIN. Though it does mean — (*He hesitates*.) you might not have a magazine to publish them in. I'm sorry, I only meant — you know — anyway he probably couldn't have done anything at that meeting. *This* is the one that counts.

STUART. What time are you seeing him?

MARTIN. What?

STUART. What time are you seeing Peter?

MARTIN. But I'm not seeing him. Except when he comes here, of course. But he doesn't know I'll be here.

STUART. You didn't make an arrangement with him? For this afternoon, or for lunch — ?

MARTIN. Absolutely not, I haven't spoken to him for weeks.

STUART (*slumps back in despair*). Oh God!

MARTIN. Why?

STUART. Because when I 'phoned Oxford this morning to make sure he'd at least left, I got Sonia, who said he hadn't mentioned anything about the Arts Council, only about meeting you to discuss a book you'd asked him to write. About the role of sex in nineteenth century politics.

MARTIN. I haven't asked him to write a book.

STUART. No, of course you haven't. So he's coming to London to meet some bloody girl. He must have forgotten the Arts Council entirely, mustn't he?

MARTIN. Well, I don't quite see —

STUART. He made you his alibi. Which means he didn't remember he already had an alibi. Which was me. So he's not there. Do you know exactly how many enemies I've got on the magazine panel?

MARTIN. Well, I know your reputation for integrity —

STUART. I think I'll kill him. Yes. Kill him. The lengths I went to, to get him co-opted on the panel. And the stuff I sent him — everything. Articles, poems, the six Hubert Parkins, some of them I didn't even have time to get xeroxed — all of it stuffed into his briefcase, under some bloody girl's bed at this very minute. Or at his feet in a pub. My representative! I should have got Humphry! Why didn't I get Humphry?

MARTIN. Well, actually, because Humphry's too trenchant for the Arts Council, you thought. And you were right. They'd have hated him. You made the right choice in Peter. Apart from his not turning up. If he doesn't.

STUART. Oh, he won't. The jig's up then, isn't it? After seven years — nine years if you count the time at Cambridge — of continuous struggle, may I be presumptuous enough to call it? Struggle? The jig's up.

MARTIN (*after slight pause*). No, it isn't. Not if you come in with me. Come in and work with me.

STUART. With you?

MARTIN. Yes.

STUART. Don't you mean Haylife and Forling's? How will that save the magazine?

MARTIN. No, I don't mean Haylife and Forling's. I mean with me, Stuart. (*Little pause.*) I've quit Haylife. And Forling too, come to that, he's far worse. (*He gives a little laugh.*) Or rather, I'm just about to quit them both. I'm going to set up on my own, which is what I always intended. I've always had the capital, and now I've got the experience. Look, Stuart, the reason I phoned you at the flat last night was that I wanted to discuss it with you. Partners, you see. You would commission and edit the fiction and the poetry. I'd do the business side and any editorial hack-work. I've learnt an enormous amount at Haylife and Forling's, I really have. I'm ready. (*Little pause.*) And the point is, we'd keep the *New Literary Review* going. As our subsidiary. (*Little pause.*) What do you think?

STUART. Subsidiary?

MARTIN. At least we'd manage without the Arts Council. And I know how much you'd like that, you've always said that they only give it out so that they have something to take away when it really matters.

Little pause.

MARTIN. And you could move back with Marigold. The two of you could live, well, you know, like a couple at last. As I know you've always wanted. Especially with a baby coming.

STUART (*after a little pause*). How did you know about that?

MARTIN. Oh, well I had lunch with Marigold last week, you see. The day after she found out she was expecting, you see.

STUART. She's not expecting. She's merely pregnant. (*Little pause.*) I wonder why she didn't tell me. About your having lunch, I mean. Not about being merely pregnant.

MARTIN. Actually, because I asked her not to. You see, I wanted to know what she thought you'd feel about the prospect of coming in with me. But I didn't want to press ahead with you until I'd, well, sorted a few things out. Which I now have, actually. And was in a position to make you what they call (*Slight laugh.*) a formal proposal. Which I now am. You see? (*Little laugh. Little pause.*) Stuart —

STUART. And what did she think I'd feel?

MARTIN. Well, to be honest, she refused to say. Because it had to be your decision. That's all she wanted. But Stuart, look —

STUART. I wonder why — (*He stops.*)

MARTIN. What?

STUART. Why she told you she was pregnant. We'd agreed not

to make it public. Until we'd made up our minds.

MARTIN. I expect because of Samantha. She's pregnant too. Didn't I tell you?

STUART. No. Congratulations. (*Ironically*.)

MARTIN (*laughs*). Thank you. It's probably the only pregnancy I'll allow her poor thing, before getting her done. She should litter in about a week. And I offered Marigold a tabby, if there is one, because she adores tabbies, as you know — Marigold — I mean, not Samantha, though Samantha seems to adore them too, at least the one I hope is the father. He was hanging around at the right time. A real rogue.

There is a pause.

STUART. So you and Marigold were just swapping pregnancy gossip?

MARTIN. Oh no. Sorry. No. The point is that I started to tell Marigold about Samantha, rabbiting on in that — that boring way of mine when on cats. And she suddenly well, broke down — Marigold — and told me she was pregnant. And then asked me not to tell you she'd told me. Because of your agreement. (*Little pause*.) So I'd rather you didn't tell her.

STUART. Tell her that you've told me that she told you? But how can I? As she only told you during a lunch you'd told her not to tell me you were having.

MARTIN. Quite. (*He laughs*.)

STUART *smiles*.

So therefore — therefore — I can't tell you how passionately she, well, seems to want to have the baby, can I?

STUART. Under the circumstances, no you can't. But then you don't have to. As I know. These things tend to slip out, between long-established couples.

MARTIN (*nods*). Sorry. (*Little pause*.) Well then. What do you think? About our setting up as partners in publishing. Keeping the *New Literary Review* going?

STUART. Thanks. *Really* thanks, Martin but I'm going to try and keep it afloat and independent even if Peter and the Arts Council let us down. I've always believed that editing it was a full-time job. Even when it's failing to appear. I haven't forgotten that I owe you quite a lot of money, by the way.

MARTIN. The money was a gift to the magazine. You know how much I want it to survive.

STUART. Yes I do. So do I. Want it to survive. But not as a subsidiary to something else, you see.

MARTIN. Does that include Marigold and the baby? Sorry, sorry, none of my business, but — well, it'll break her heart —

The sound of footsteps, off, coming up the stairs.

HUMPHRY (*enters*). What's going on, this room reeks of passion, in the famous phrase. What have you two been up to?

MARTIN. We're waiting for Peter.

STUART. Although we suspect he's forgotten to come.

HUMPHRY. I doubt it. Is this all there is? (*Surveying the opened wine bottles.*)

MARTIN. No, there's some here. (*Handing him a bottle.*)

STUART. Why do you doubt it? After the way you've been talking about him recently.

HUMPHRY. I doubt it because I saw him two days ago when I went to give a paper at Oxford. I had dinner with him. And Sonia. And their babies. He boasted that he was coming down here this morning to do what he called your street-fighting for you. Why do you think I'm here, if not to observe you in crisis and triumph. You're handling the crisis part badly, let's hope you come up to snuff in the triumph part.

STUART. And you in the disaster part. Tell him.

MARTIN. Well, there's a possibility that he's merely coming to London for his usual — um —

STUART. Fuck.

HUMPHRY. Of course he is. He'd go anywhere and do anything for a fuck. Including even attending an Arts Council meeting on your behalf.

MARTIN. Yes, but you see — he lied to Sonia about why he was coming up to London, he told her he was coming to see me to discuss a book, which isn't true, instead of saying he was going to the meeting, which would have been true, and the obvious lie to tell, because at least it would have been true, if he remembered it. If you follow.

HUMPHRY. Of course I follow. Merely because you can't speak properly doesn't mean I can't understand you. Generally well before you're finished. I suppose you got all this from Sonia?

MARTIN. Well, not about coming for the fuck.

HUMPHRY. The reason he lied to Sonia was that it was simpler and less fatiguing than telling her the truth. Have you tried talking to that woman recently? A simple statement from you is followed by an imbecile question from her, and she doesn't stop until your statements have become as imbecile as her questions, in a ghastly parody of the Socratic dialogue. Then, as you sit drained of ideas, energy, humanity, she changes a nappy in front of you. Virtually all over you, in fact. He had absolutely no right to marry her. Getting her pregnant was no excuse. We should have talked him out of it. It was our duty. Or talked Nick into taking his place. He's got nothing particularly important to do with his life and they'd have got on perfectly. Her pathological need to ask imbecile questions would actually give a purpose to his pathological need to tell lies. (*To* MARTIN.) Do you follow?

MARTIN. I think so.

HUMPHRY. Explain it back to me, then?

MARTIN. It was easier to say he was coming to see me than to explain about the Arts Council, the magazine, grants, etc, and Stuart.

HUMPHRY. Exactly. Furthermore he won't let you down because a) he's a good and loyal friend, b) he actually longs to crusade on your behalf because c) he's got nothing better to do. And he's only twenty-eight. Unlike Nick he actually had a mind, a few years back. What'll he be like when he's forty? Probably exactly the same only less so, having less energy to be it with.

MARTIN. Yes.

STUART. What?

MARTIN. I think Humpty's got it right, as usual.

STUART. Then why isn't he here? He's now actually late. Or 'phoned?

HUMPHRY. Wait thou child of hope. For time will give thee all things. Except a decent glass of wine ever, at least here. This is simultaneously bland and acid, is it English?

MARTIN. It's a Chablis, a vintage isn't it? That's what they said —

HUMPHRY (*goes to shelf, pours himself stale wine*). How's Marigold?

STUART. In Cheltenham. Visiting her mother. She's ill.

MARTIN. Her father.

STUART. Yes.

HUMPHRY. Odd how Martin always seems to know more about your life than you do. Perhaps it's because he takes a greater interest. Anyway, you're all right are you, you two?

STUART. Which two?

HUMPHRY. You and Marigold.

STUART. Why?

HUMPHRY. Because I 'phoned you last night to say I was coming down and got an exceptionally loquacious Indian girl, from the sound of her, who gave me the distinct impression that you and Marigold were no longer living together. Although I can't be sure. Her rhythms got in the way of her sense.

STUART *says nothing.*

MARTIN. It's only a financial arrangement — um —

STUART. As a matter of fact she's pregnant. And we're going to get married.

MARTIN *looks at him.*

HUMPHRY (*after a little pause*). Good.

STUART. Really? You don't think we have a duty to talk me out of it? Or get Nick to take my place?

HUMPHRY. Don't be ridiculous. I've got the greatest admiration for Marigold, as you know.

STUART. Because she's got a fine mind?

HUMPHRY. No, she hasn't. But when it comes to the things that matter she's got a mind of her own, which is more important. Congratulations.

STUART *nods.*

And now to a vastly more passionate relationship. How's Samantha? Kindly confine your reply to two sentences.

MARTIN. She's pregnant. But we're not going to get married. What about you?

HUMPHRY. I'm not pregnant. And I wouldn't dream of getting married, even if I were. But I've moved into your old rooms at last. (*To* STUART.) I've always wanted them, but that ridiculous Scot who lived above you took them over when he got his fellowship and so I'd given up hope. But last month he committed suicide. Quite upsetting isn't it? I mean, people we convert into jokes have an obligation not to do that sort of thing. He was a mathematical genius apparently, but his creative juices dried up suddenly. As they tend to with mathematicians, they finish young. Actually he must have been rather short on real personality, in spite of his bluster. As he hasn't left the trace of a ghost behind. Even in the bedroom, where he did it with a razor. I haven't even bothered to have it redecorated. The odd thing is that I feel I'm finally where I always intended to be. At home, in other words. So much so that this morning I rose at six, walked twice round Great Court, and wrote the first fourteen and a half lines of my book on Wagner. (*Little pause.*) But, nothing of consequence. At least in *your* life-enhancing terms.

The sound of footsteps running up the stairs.

MARTIN. That must be Peter.

There is a sudden explosive cough.

HUMPHRY. No, it isn't.

> STUART *groans slightly.*

> NICK *enters. He stands for a moment, a cigarette between his lips, then begins to cough again. The cough becomes explosive, the cigarette shoots out and lands — preferably — on* STUART's *desk.*

NICK (*pulling himself together*). That does it! I'm giving up taxis. The way that shit took the corner, my bum skidding, my stomach churning, my head pounding, God, I wish I'd thrown up. All over the back of his neck. It was red with ginger hair on it.

> MARTIN *hands him back his cigarette.*

NICK. Thanks. (*He continues to smoke it.*)

MARTIN. Where were you coming from?

NICK. Don't know. Earls Court it looked like. Some girl picked me up at the French pub last night, took me back to her place. At least I hope it was a girl. Had her back to me when I woke up. Had a girl's spine. Smelt like a girl. But snoring like a man. So it was either an Australian or a hermaphrodite or both. The haunting question is whether I poked it, I keep recalling a brief spasm during the night. I hope it was just my cough. News from Peter?

MARTIN. We're waiting.

NICK. Oh, well I've only a few minutes — but don't worry. It's in the bag.

HUMPHRY. Nicholas's confidence is the first real alarm signal.

NICK. Hey, Humpty, what's all this I've been hearing? About you.

HUMPHRY. What have you been hearing?

NICK. About your lethal effect on the undergraduate sensibility, and — (*Seeing something in* HUMPHRY's *face, changing tack.*) other tittle tattle, very complimentary about you as an intellectual glamour-figure because of your lectures and stuff, from Harrop. He went up to do a poetry reading recently, he was in the French pub last night and do you know what he claims, that he's won the Cheltenham prize. For that nappy full of homosexless verse he dropped last year.

MARTIN. Well, he has, hasn't he?

NICK. How do you know, he told me he wasn't allowed to tell anyone until the announcement.

STUART. I was one of the judges. In fact I voted for him.

NICK. You didn't tell me.

STUART. No, well I'm not allowed to tell anyone either.

NICK. But how could you vote for Harrop? You know I loathe him.

STUART. I didn't vote for him. I voted for his poems. Why are you so sure it's in the bag?

NICK. What? Oh, your grant, because Peter told me.

STUART. When?

NICK (*being watched closely by* HUMPHRY). Last night. He 'phoned to say he was coming to London for the meeting, what about lunch afterwards, along with the rest of us, he couldn't get hold of you, just a foreign girl at your flat, but I can't make it because I'm having lunch with *Vogue,* to discuss doing a series of articles on this and that, but he said, *en passant,* the grant was in the bag. (*He coughs violently.*)

HUMPHRY. That's aesthetically one of the least attractive ways of killing yourself, Nicholas, why don't you stop it?

NICK. Yes. Well I will. I've got to go. Love to Peter, sorry I missed him — oh Martin, I think I'd better not, I'm too young to settle down, and also they turn into cats, and I'm less soppy about those. (*He goes to the door and stops.*) Oh God, I almost forgot — that article I sent you, reviewing the reviewers sort of thing? I don't suppose you've had a chance to read it yet?

STUART. No, not properly. I've looked at it of course, but I haven't — (*He gestures.*)

NICK. No, that's all right, but can I have it back for a while! I'm not really happy with some sections of it, especially the couple of pages on Angela Thark, for instance, I didn't know she was dying when I wrote it, don't forget. I'd like to be more — more delicate. Cut out the bit about her blood-soaked prose, etc, and get at some of the reviewers for not admiring her more — she's got that daughter, after all. Grieving friends. I'm one myself, in a way.

STUART *has gone to his desk and is looking for the manuscript.*

MARTIN. Really, I thought you couldn't stand her?

NICK. That was only when she was alive. (*He gives a little laugh.*) Death brings its own respect, and besides I won't have to see her again. (*Laughs again.*) All right. Of course I couldn't stand her. Although I always maintained that she was sexy. The point is I can't let it go as it stands. It makes me seem a brute. Which I am, about her. But I can't afford to seem it, can I?

STUART. I can't find it. Can you work from your own copy? (*Still looking.*)

NICK. No, I can't. I destroyed it. I lost a bit of confidence in it, you see, when you went on failing to mention it every time I saw you. Not that I'm blaming you. I destroyed a lot of other stuff too. Although I sometimes wonder whether you realise what an influence you have, Stuart. Your approval. Doesn't he? Any luck? (*To* STUART.)

STUART. No, but it's here somewhere.

NICK (*conscious that* HUMPHRY *is watching him*). You know I'm beginning to wonder whether I'm really cut out for a career in literature. I find writing even more of a chore than fucking. And a lot of the people one meets are even worse. Actually, I wish I were a vicar. With a wife, a bike, a dog and some children. And a little bit of faith. And a private income, of course. Two private incomes in fact.

HUMPHRY. What I can't work out is why?

NICK. What?

HUMPHRY. Why you're lying. Nicholas. Your motive. Or are you just keeping in practice.

MARTIN. You don't think by any chance —

NICK. What?

MARTIN. Well, I mean — you wouldn't have sold it to somebody else, would you? I mean — no, I'm sorry. Of course not.

HUMPHRY. *Vogue,* of course!

NICK. What?

HUMPHRY. Nicholas has sold it to *Vogue.* Well done. (*To* MARTIN.)

NICK. Oh come on! (*Little pause.*) Yes, well actually what happened is that I sent my copy to my agent, and she showed it to *Vogue,* without my consent, naturally, and it turned out that *Vogue* was thinking of doing a piece along my lines.

STUART. My lines, as a matter of fact. As I suggested them.

NICK. Yes, well they're hardly original, are they? It's how it's done that matters. Not that *Vogue* wants it as it stands. It's got to be spiced up, with little character-sketches and assassinations thrown in, illustrated with cartoons and fish-eye photographs. I've already worked out something for Harrop. It won't be the same article at all, in the end. No reason why they shouldn't be published in both. Eh?

HUMPHRY. Then you don't need Stuart's copy back, do you? You can get one from *Vogue.*

NICK. Yes, well my agent says she doesn't like the thought of it being offered to two different magazines at the same time. She says it's unethical.

STUART, MARTIN *and* HUMPHRY *laugh.*

Perhaps. But bloody hell, I'm a professional literary journalist. I live by what I sell. And you didn't bother to acknowledge receiving it, let alone let me know what you thought about it. And I've waited for years for you to ask me to contribute something — and the fact is, it could lie rotting away on your desk for ever. The magazine's failed to come out twice running now, and there's a decent chance it'll never come out again.

A pause.

STUART. A decent chance, is it?

NICK. According to Peter.

STUART. According to Peter when?

NICK. This morning. He stopped in for a cup of coffee on his way to the meeting.

STUART. But you were coming from an Australian or a hermaphrodite in Earls Court this morning.

HUMPHRY. Whom you either poked or coughed into.

NICK. Yes. Well that must have been yesterday morning. In fact, it sounds like all my yesterday mornings recently. Except tomorrow's. When I'll have had coffee with Peter. Won't I? (*He attempts a laugh, coughs instead.*)

STUART. And what precisely did he say? About the grant?

NICK. Yes, well — apparently the whole Arts Council panel, virtually, thinks you're elitist. He's going to do his best, but he reckons you're finished. But knowing you you'll struggle on for years, editing a magazine that never comes out at all. And I'll have missed the chance of a deal with *Vogue*. And I need it. Can I have the article please?

STUART. Actually no, you can't. I must have stuck it in with the material I gave Peter to show the Arts Council. So it was probably sitting in that calf-skin briefcase of his when you had coffee with him. But don't worry, Nick, I shan't publish it. The truth is I've been wondering how to return it to you without hurting you. All you had to do was to say straight out that *Vogue* wanted it, did I mind? I'd have been delighted. It's perfect for *Vogue*. Just as it stands. None of this need have happened.

NICK. Yes — well they're right. You *are* elitist.

STUART. Well, somebody's got to be, haven't they? Especially at a time when nobody else wants to be.

NICK. But they don't want *you* to be, either. Do they? So whatever you think about me the magazine's finished. And the truth is, actually, that I'm sorry. But I think you should face it, and not waste your life —

MARIGOLD *enters.*

HUMPHRY. Marigold.

MARIGOLD. Hello Humpty, I didn't know you were coming down.

NICK. Hi, Marigold.

MARTIN. How's your mother?

MARIGOLD. Terrific. Apart from being dead, that is. It's my father I went to see. They've discovered he's got what he calls a bum ticker, so he'll have to give up all the things he really lives for, scotch, cigarettes and furtive little forays to London. To balance that, he's got to give up his work too, which he's always hated.

NICK. He's a doctor, isn't he?

MARIGOLD. No a vicar.

HUMPHRY. Oh. Then Nicholas, you should meet him. Nicholas is thinking of taking orders aren't you, Nicholas? He has some of the right qualifications. He lies badly about things that don't matter.

NICK (*attempts a laugh*). Yes, well — I'd better be — oh those remedial students of yours — how are they doing?

MARIGOLD. Very well. By next term they should have made me completely illiterate, what have you been up to?

NICK. What?

MARIGOLD. You look shiftier than usual, even.

HUMPHRY. Come on, Nicholas, tell her.

NICK. Oh come on — look, I've really got to go, I'm late. See you all then. (*He exits coughing.*)

MARIGOLD. What's he done? Something uniquely disgusting?

STUART. Not really. Merely withdrawn his unwanted article on inconsequential literary figures of our time.

MARIGOLD. But that's good, isn't it? You were agonising over how to tell him.

STUART. It was the way he did it, Nick being Nick.

HUMPHRY. Of course you realise he only did it that way and sold it to *Vogue*, if he *has* sold it to *Vogue*, because he wanted to spare himself the humiliation of your rejecting him. Which he nevertheless still managed to achieve, Nicholas being Nicholas. Good to hear about the baby though, but that doesn't mean you have to marry him, you know?

MARIGOLD (*laughs*). Thank you, but where's the roving boy, I thought he was meant to be here by now?

STUART. We think he may not make it, but it doesn't matter, as he sent a message via Nick. We're not getting our grant doubled. On the grounds that we're elitist.

MARIGOLD (*after a little pause*). Elitist!

STUART. Actually, let's face it, or let me face it, at last. It's probably the right decision. The fact is that the magazine doesn't really matter, to anyone except me. As Nick pointed out. (*Little laugh.*) To do him credit.

MARIGOLD. Yes, it does. It matters to lots of people. Hubert Parkin among them. Or he wouldn't have given you his six new poems, would he?

STUART. He only gave them to me because I gave him that bloody party, which was finally what bankrupted us, as Martin has always refrained from pointing out, although he came close a little while ago. Anyway, the Parkins will get themselves published somewhere far more public, and for real money, instead of promises of it.

MARIGOLD. But you're not seriously talking of giving up! Not now! You can't. He can't, can he?

STUART. Oh, yes I can.

MARIGOLD. But — but it's not fair. (*She gives a little laugh.*) It's actually not fair.

STUART. Being fair has nothing to do with it. The printers want their money, and why shouldn't they have it, they've worked for it? The landlord wants his rent, and why shouldn't he have it, he owns the place? I can't pay the telephone bill, the electricity bill, I can't even pay for the issues of the magazine I fail to bring out. If fair means anything it's not fair on them. And above all it's not fair on you. It probably never has been. But certainly not now. Come on, Humpty. Let's hear the truth.

HUMPHRY. But you've just spoken it. Almost. Even if you get the grant doubled you'll be having a version of this conversation a baby or two from now.

STUART. Yes, well trust Humpty to go the unpalatable stage further. But he's right. In the end it won't survive.

MARTIN. It will. If you come in with me —

MARIGOLD. You don't know everything! You don't always know everything! (*To* HUMPHRY.)

HUMPHRY *looks at her, makes to speak, doesn't.*

MARIGOLD. I — can I — look, do you mind if I — well I want to talk to our editor, the literary gent, you see. Sorry. (*Little laugh*.)

HUMPHRY. Of course. (*He hesitates, takes* MARIGOLD's *hand, kisses it.*)

MARTIN (*to* STUART). Look, do please think about what I said. (*To* MARIGOLD.) Get him to think about it. (*He follows* HUMPHRY *to the door, makes to speak again, then follows* HUMPHRY *out.*)

A pause.

MARIGOLD. I don't want you to give it up, you see. Not now. Especially not now. Not for me, even. Not for anything. You'd be lost without it. And you'd make a nonsense of everything — I — we —

STUART. No, I wouldn't. Realising that's a relief. The fact is, I'd be lost without you. Which, in a sense, old Martin did point out. (*Little laugh*.) I want the baby. The feeling has been growing in my bones all morning. It became an absolute certainty when I announced your pregnancy to Humpty. In a slightly rasping manner, I admit. So, in the phrase. Forget literature. Start life, eh? Old life itself.

MARIGOLD. Yes, well there's a slight irony here. Of the sort that usually only turns up in literature. There isn't a baby anymore. Actually. I stopped off on my way up to Cheltenham. In fact the reason I went up to Cheltenham was to stop off on the way up there. It went without a hitch. You'll be glad to hear.

STUART. But — but — I thought we'd agreed — that — we were going to think about it. We had time — we gave ourselves three weeks.

MARIGOLD. Yes, well, when it came to it I decided I wasn't being — fair. I want you, you see, and you and the magazine have always come together, haven't you, and I didn't really know how we could make room for anything else. Anyway it's done. Sorry.

STUART (*after a little pause*). My fault. I should have known what I really wanted a little earlier, shouldn't I? (*He goes to her.*) Well, we'll just have to start again. Now we both know what I really want.

The sound of footsteps on the stairs, very fast, door flings open.

PETER (*enters*). Christ, these stairs! Marigold! (*He goes to her, kisses her on the cheek, looks at them triumphantly.*) What it comes to is this! They'll guarantee all your costs, undertake to clear all your outstanding debts, pay your rent and provide you with a marginally above-the-dole salary, plus bona fide expenses. Such as the occasional fling for the likes of Hubert Parkin. Which is, I think, substantially more than you expected, being equivalent to a trebled rather than doubled grant, eh? And so considerably more than I thought we had a hope in hell of getting. Oh, I know it's not enough to live and breed on, but going by my own experience, who wants to do that? (*He laughs.*) And there was a lot of resistance, I told old

Nick there would be, they're such shits! All some of those salaried buggers with pensions to come wanted to discuss was whether you were elitist. Thank God for old Nick, eh? His article was crucial.

STUART. Really? (*He laughs*.) How perfect.

PETER. They hadn't realised the direction you wanted to go in until I read it out, and I didn't even know I had it until I was speeding towards them in my taxi after coffee with Nick. It just happened to be the first thing I plucked out of my briefcase. All that stuff about Angela Twerk —

STUART. Thark.

PETER. Yes, had them falling about. Except for the routine po-face from Nottingham University, but they all hate her anyway, so she actually helped the cause. And those Belfast poets too, Dougan and O' — O' —

STUART. Leary. Though actually it's Leary and O'Dougan.

PETER. Yes, they liked them for their directness, their simplicity, their brutal rhymes and vocabulary, their — their — sing-song —

STUART. Lack of talent.

PETER. Yes.

STUART (*to* MARIGOLD). They were in the wrong bundle. I thought I'd sent them back.

PETER. Well, don't. As far as the Arts Council was concerned, that one about shit exploding in our faces made up for all the Hubert Parkins, which they loathed on the grounds that they were — were —

STUART. Poems.

PETER. Yes. What were they about anyway? Has the old bugger gone permanently around the twist?

STUART. No.

PETER. You sure?

STUART. No, not any more. Most of them are about death.

Four — three — no, four are great poems. In my view. Which is
not to say he hasn't gone around the twist. (*With effort.*)
Peter, look, thanks a lot, but the thing is —

PETER. No. I enjoyed it, arguing for literature and critical
standards brought back the old Cambridge days. I sometimes
wonder whether Oxford isn't addling my brain, and what
could be nicer than paying out large sums of taxpayers' money
to one's chums, against the odds. And perverts on the Arts
Council. There were nine of them, I calculated three queers,
three not, three nothing. (*He laughs.*) God, you look ravishing.
(*To* MARIGOLD.) But you always do. If distraught. Are you
distraught?

MARIGOLD. No, perfectly um, traught, thanks.

PETER. Did Nick show up?

STUART. For a few moments.

PETER. I was worried I might have given him a too feeble
impression of our chances, but I hadn't read his article. Tell
him my congratulations and sorry about lunch.

STUART. Yes.

PETER. Where are Humpty and Martin, I was sure they'd be
here? Especially Martin. Were they?

STUART. Yes. But they had to go.

PETER. Humpty came over to read a paper a few weeks ago, very
trenchant and hateable, was the general view, on Hegel,
Nietzsche and Wagner, but we had a nice dinner, scarcely ever
seen him so relaxed and charming, but Sonia brings out the
best in him, they seem to have a rapport, partly because she
doesn't think too highly of his intellect, he likes that, can I
use the 'phone? (*Going to it.*)

STUART. Of course.

PETER (*dialling*). If by any unlikely chance Sonia should take
it into her head to ring — who *is* that in your flat, by the way,
is she foreign or what?

MARIGOLD. Yes, she's from Surrey, Godalming in fact. A

teacher from my school.

PETER. Oh, sounded middle-Eastern to me. Anyway, could you explain — (*Dialling again.*) that I've got an arrangement with Martin about a book, though she knows about that, and then I'm hoping to meet up with Nick for an early drink, and then Humphry for a late one, and then dinner with Stuart and Martin, and if I'm not back on the late train, I'll be spending the night in one of Martin's spare rooms, and I'll be back on one of the morning trains. Or lunch time, about? (*Little pause, grins.*) What's called tit for tat. Not that the magazine's tat, (*He laughs.*) but I'm after tit. Sorry darling. (*To* MARIGOLD.)

STUART. Of course.

PETER. Is something the matter with your 'phone? (*Dials again.*) She's expecting me to call (*He looks at his watch.*) five minute ago, was our arrangement. We're having lunch and on. I've booked us into the Charing Cross Hotel. Views of the Strand at post-coital dawn and all that. (*He listens.*) No. Bugger. (*He slams the telephone down.*)

STUART. It's possible we've been cut off at last, I suppose. (*He catches* MARIGOLD'*s eye. They laugh slightly.*)

Lights.

Curtain.

ACT TWO

Scene One

STUART's *and* MARTIN's *office. Eight years ago. Late afternoon. The office is transformed, painted and orderly.* STUART *still has the same desk, in the same position. Opposite is* MARTIN's *desk, slightly smaller than* STUART's, *but more antique. On both desks, a telephone. There is also a desk in the corner with a type-writer on it, a vase of flowers, some photographs propped, a secretarial desk. On the walls there are some book shelves, but now full of books, most of them evidently proofs of coffee-table style books. On the walls, covers of books on gardening, nursing, cricket, bridge, chess, various historical figures — Napoleon, Hitler, Churchill, etc, and a poster for a poetry reading, new, by Dougan and O'Leary.*

There is a new arm-chair, a new sofa, a couple of hard-backed chairs, and an elegant and antique cocktail cabinet. On MARTIN's *desk, and on the wall above his desk are photographs, drawings, cartoons, and reproductions of paintings of cats.*

MARTIN *is sitting at the secretarial desk, typing rapidly, though not professionally. He stops. Listens.*

The sound of footsteps on the stairs.

MARTIN *increases the speed of his typing, as* HUMPHRY *enters. He is carrying an overnight bag. He looks around, has trouble locating* MARTIN *in the corner as* MARTIN *hurriedly pulls out a sheet of paper.*

MARTIN. Hi, Humpty. Won't be a second. (*Scribbling his signature at the bottom of the sheet.*)

HUMPHRY. Oh. Now you're being the secretary too, are you?

MARTIN. No, it's Michelle's evening class, so I let her go home early. She has to finish *Macbeth*. Actually (*Putting the letter on the desk.*) I expect we'll have to replace her soon, she's determined to get to university.

HUMPHRY. By far the best place for her. She's not bright enough to be a secretary.

MARTIN. I know. So she'll probably end up as a publisher, in competition, I suppose. Want a drink?

HUMPHRY. A small brandy, to settle the stomach. It always tends to be a bit queasy after lunch with Nick.

MARTIN (*going to the cocktail cabinet*). I've only got a good French one, I'm afraid, will that do? (*Extracting the bottle, pouring.*) What's he up to, we haven't seen him for a few weeks, Nick.

HUMPHRY. You might see him later. He said he'd look in. But only if he gets his television job presenting some new BBC books programme.

MARTIN. Yes, we heard about that. Lots of competition, one gathers.

HUMPHRY. A half a dozen equally trivial creatures. He's worried about the balding, portly poet figure, the one he calls Nappies.

MARTIN. Oh yes, Harrop. I've never understood why he hates him so much.

HUMPHRY. Because they're soul mates, of course. I keep expecting you to move office. Aren't you getting cramped?

MARTIN. A little. But Stuart's very attached — and had a few financial entanglements with the landlord — so it's probably wiser to stay on. For the moment anyway.

HUMPHRY. Where is he? Stuart.

MARTIN. At the printers. It's his turn. He hates doing it, but he insists.

HUMPHRY. How's Marigold?

MARTIN. We're just waiting to hear if she's going to be made Assistant Headmistress. The interview's this afternoon. Where are you going by the way? Or are you staying overnight?

HUMPHRY. No, I'm passing through to Exeter to see my parents, so I haven't got too long.

MARTIN. They're still in decent fettle, are they?

HUMPHRY. It's his seventy-fifth birthday tomorrow, but he's
OK. I've brought along a sweater I cut a hole in for my mother
to darn. So she'll be OK too. I've also brought along a book
by Edwina McClusky, on Plato, which they won't understand,
which is just as well, as it's mainly wrong. But it'll support
my boast that she and I are having a romance. So it'll do
someone some good, won't it? McClusky on Plato.

MARTIN. But Dr McClusky's in her seventies, isn't she?

HUMPHRY. Yes, but they don't know that. And I hope they
don't find out or they'll think there's something wrong with
me. All they know is that she's an older woman. Which
worries them a little. Which is exactly the right amount, for
parents of their age, with a son of my type. And that'll be
balanced out by the news that I've been appointed Senior
Moral Tutor. Did we ever bump into one of those in our day?
Apparently their job was to advise us on all our little
problems, financial and especially emotional, a sort of uncle
figure, with a cutting edge. I'm certainly the first one I've
ever come across.

MARTIN. But you'll enjoy it won't you?

HUMPHRY. I'm afraid I probably will. Well Martin?

MARTIN. How's the brandy?

HUMPHRY. I hadn't noticed. Probably a good sign. Come
on then. What do you want?

MARTIN. Why do you think I want something?

HUMPHRY. Because when you 'phoned to ask when I was next
coming down, and I said today, you said good, please come
and see us. But you didn't say Stuart wouldn't be here. You
and I don't usually end up in the same room, unless Stuart's
present. Do we? So it must be something you want. And
probably don't want Stuart to know about. Is it?

MARTIN. I sometimes wonder whether you enjoy knowing so
much. Yes. If it weren't Stuart's afternoon at the printers, I'd

have suggested meeting somewhere else. Have you — well, have you committed your book on Wagner to a publisher, yet?

HUMPHRY. No.

MARTIN. Would you consider committing it to us?

HUMPHRY. To make up one of your coffee table specials, a short and breezy life padded out with photographs and facsimiles?

MARTIN (*laughs. There is a small pause*). Yes, well I expected you'd think that. But actually I was hoping you'd do us the honour of being our first real book. Of scholarship, judgement and imagination. As we all know it will be. To usher in our next phase. It can be as long as you like, and have no illustrations at all, if you prefer. Two, three, even four volumes. (*Slight pause.*) Three anyway. (*He laughs.*)

HUMPHRY. And you haven't talked to Stuart about it?

MARTIN. No.

HUMPHRY. Why not?

MARTIN. Because I want it to be a surprise. He'd be your editor, you see. Would you like that?

HUMPHRY. Yes.

MARTIN. Terrific! We'll draw up a contract, then —

HUMPHRY. No, we won't. The slight catch, from all our points of view, is that I'm not writing a book on Wagner. I abandoned it about three weeks ago, if May the seventeenth, at three in the morning, was about three weeks ago.

MARTIN. But why, Humpty? The last time I was in Cambridge I saw how much you'd done. There were what? Three hundred pages already on your desk.

HUMPHRY (*looks at him, smiles slightly*). You counted them, did you? While I was out of the room?

MARTIN. Oh come on, Humpty. I'm a publisher. I could see at a glance how far you'd got. You mustn't give it up. You mustn't.

HUMPHRY. Yes, I must. I've got the scholarship, and the judgement, but not the imagination to understand him. Him in relation to his music. Everything I've written about him reduces him to my own sort of size. Which makes him too small to be interesting to me. I appear to have an instinctive and ineradicable tendency to diminish what I most admire.

MARTIN. I can see you're going through some sort of — dark night of the soul, but — well, what about a monograph? If not on Wagner, somebody else. What about publishing your fellow-ship dissertation?

HUMPHRY. It's on Hegel, Martin. In German mostly. I stopped believing in it before I began it. I went through with it because I thought I wanted a Fellowship because it would allow me to work on the things I loved. Which I want to go on loving. Which is why I won't allow my intelligence to fix on them, ever again. I don't think I can be simpler, even for you.

MARTIN. I'm being selfish. I'm sorry.

HUMPHRY. You're being selfish for Stuart, as usual. I'm sorry. I expect it's all far harder for you than for me.

MARTIN (*looks at him*). No, I'm actually very happy. (*Little pause.*) Really. If that's what you mean. Although you're right, I'm sometimes not sure what you mean, being simple. (*He laughs.*)

HUMPHRY. He doesn't know, then?

MARTIN. Know what?

HUMPHRY. Don't be alarmed. (*Little pause.*) It's not my business.

MARTIN. Thank you.

HUMPHRY. Our lives aren't dissimilar. In spite of appearances on the one hand, and reality on the other. Can I give you some advice?

MARTIN (*thinks*). No. Really Humpty, thanks. I respect you far too much. I might listen to it, you see. And then I'd have nothing. Nothing I want, anyway.

The sound of footsteps on the stairs. Coughing.

HUMPHRY. Nick. He's got the job, then?

Cough, off, followed by a sneeze.

HUMPHRY. But do we want that sound on our screens, even though it's better than what he'll have to say, about books?

As other coughs and sneezes follow.

PETER (*enters*). Don't you ever get your bloody stairs swept? Humpty, how are you? It's been ages.

HUMPHRY. Peter.

PETER. Stuart not here, then?

MARTIN. No, it's his turn at the printers, I didn't know you were coming in today.

PETER. Nor did I, but I had to, as it turned out, I 'phoned you from Oxford station and Paddington, but of course none of the bloody boxes took my money, pumped it straight through and onto the floor. But anyway you're here. Thank God. And here's this, two weeks of exhaustion and only a month overdue. (*Slapping a typescript down on the table.*) As promised. About forty thousand words I worked it out at on the train, which is only twenty-five thousand fewer than we agreed. But I checked some of the other coffee tables at Blackwell's the other day, most of them get away with fifty-five thousand, so if we add an extra dozen pictures — who's doing the pictures by the way? I'm looking forward to seeing what she's got.

MARTIN. Well, I think you are actually, aren't you?

PETER. Am I, bugger!

MARTIN. Yes, well that's what we put in the contract. Anyway, you've done it, wonderful.

HUMPHRY. What's it on?

PETER. The great religious leaders of world history, Mahommed, Buddha, Jesus, you'll probably think I skimped on Jesus, just a few thousand, as a matter of fact, but then let's face it, he's being over-done at the moment, he's always being over-done, in fact, but I'll pad him out if you think it necessary, and there's a whole chapter (*To* HUMPHRY.) on Wagner, in the myth-creator section, out of deference to you. You're in the index. And the acknowledgements, Humpty.

HUMPHRY. Thank you. Why do you do it?

PETER. What?

HUMPHRY. Go on turning out books, like this?

PETER. Because I've got four children. Why do you think?

MARTIN. Um, even with pictures I've got a feeling that forty-five thousand might be a trifle on the short side —

PETER. Yes, yes, well the thing is I've got to get on up to Hampstead fairly quickly, can we go into this next time I'm here, or you or/and Stuart are in Oxford. The really crucial question is whether Sonia and I can have dinner with you tonight, preferably at your place?

MARTIN. Oh, I'm sorry. Not really, I'm afraid. Not tonight.

PETER. Why not?

MARTIN. Because I'm going out to dinner.

PETER. Can't we come too?

MARTIN. Well, not really. You see, they happen to be people I don't know. Well, I mean.

PETER. Then cancel.

MARTIN. Oh no. I couldn't do that. They've gone to a lot of trouble. (*Little pause.*) They're an elderly couple, you see, who've just moved into the basement flat. They're going to be the new caretakers. They're Greeks, so it'll be all ritual and no surprises. Like unexpected guests (*He laughs.*) and probably a ghastly evening, but I couldn't let them down, could I?

PETER. Oh Christ! Sonia's had to make arrangements for somebody to look after the children, on the understanding that she'd be having dinner with you.

MARTIN. But what understanding?

HUMPHRY. He means you were his alibi and it's all gone wrong, at last.

PETER. Exactly. I told her I was having dinner with you and then I'd probably stay overnight in one of your extra rooms. I always say that nowadays, when I'm coming to London, it saves work. But just as I was leaving she took it into her head — the first time ever. Ever! — that she wanted to come.

HUMPHRY *laughs slightly*.

Shut up, Humpty.

MARTIN. Well, tell her you got the day wrong. Or I did. Yes, blame me, that's the easiest.

PETER. I can't.

MARTIN. Why not?

PETER. Because she made me 'phone you to warn her there'd be one extra for dinner.

MARTIN. But you didn't 'phone me. Unless Michelle forgot —

PETER. No, of course I didn't.

HUMPHRY *laughs again*.

Will you shut up, Humpty! No, of course I didn't 'phone you. But I had to pretend to. And pretty bloody nerve-racking it was too, as Sonia was in the room when I did it. I was terrified she'd grab the 'phone out of my hand, to have a few words with you herself, you know what she's like, I was phoning somebody entirely different, of course.

MARTIN. Oh, who?

HUMPHRY. The person he'd actually arranged to have dinner with, of course.

PETER. Of course. I assumed that she'd interpret my saying Sonia was coming to dinner to mean that my dinner with her was off.

MARTIN. And did she?

PETER. No, because as it turned out, I wasn't talking to her at all. I was talking to her mother-in-law. Who'd come in to look after their two little girls. Jane had already left to do some shopping here.

MARTIN. Good heavens! What did she make of it?

PETER. Who?

HUMPHRY. Jane's mother-in-law.

PETER. No idea, as soon as I cottoned on to who was at the other end of the line I said, so we'll *both* see you at eight, looking forward to it enormously, and hung up.

MARTIN. So the mother-in-law of the girl you're having dinner with in London is expecting you and Sonia for dinner tonight in Cambridge, with, I suppose, the girl's husband, can that be right?

PETER. Oh, don't be ridiculous Martin, she hadn't the slightest idea who I was, so she doesn't know who to expect for dinner tonight, does she, so it doesn't matter. What matters is what am I going to do about Sonia, who expects to be having dinner with you. She was catching an afternoon train, so she's probably already here. She wanted a few hours for shopping too.

HUMPHRY. Who is Jane?

PETER. Oh, nobody. Just the wife of a friend.

MARTIN. Anyone we know?

PETER. No, no, his name's Papworth, Roland Papworth, a theologian at New College. But what —

HUMPHRY. Does he know what you're up to?

PETER. What?

HUMPHRY. With his wife Jane, does he know what you're up to?

PETER. Of course he doesn't, I wouldn't hurt Roland for the world, he and I have become extremely close, he gave me an enormous amount of help with *Great Religious Leaders,* for one thing, he's particularly strong on Buddha. (*To* MARTIN.) Can't you really think of anything?

MARTIN. You don't mean he wrote it?

PETER. What?

MARTIN. This Roland Papworth, the theologian, did he write it?

Your book? I need to know because of the copyright —

PETER (*exasperated*). No, of course he didn't write it, he merely filled in a bit of the history, background, ideas, that sort of thing, and the Buddha bits, but I did almost all the last draft. Of course, he's probably expecting his name on the title page, that was one of the things I wanted to discuss with you later, and he'll want a share of the royalties, but look —

MARTIN. There aren't any royalties. You get paid a fee.

PETER. Oh. Well, I thought —

MARTIN. Half of which you've already received, you see.

PETER. Yes, well, don't worry, I'll think up some way of sharing something with him.

HUMPHRY. Apart from his wife, you mean?

PETER. What?

HUMPHRY. I suppose she's good in bed, is she?

PETER. Terrific. If a bit voracious. I sometimes wonder whether old Roland's pulling his weight. But that's not the point at the moment. The point is my marriage. It's at risk.

HUMPHRY. But does that matter?

PETER (*incredulously*). Does it matter? I've got four bloody children. Do you think I want to subject them to some quite unnecessary trauma — not to speak of Sonia. It's never crossed her mind — she'd break down completely — do you think I don't care?

HUMPHRY. I know you don't care. About anything that matters.

PETER. What do you mean?

HUMPHRY. Haven't I made myself plain, even to you? That you go on spawning children and pretending to love a fatuous wife that you can't even be bothered to betray competently, while writing books on subjects that you inevitably demean.

There is a pause.

PETER *hits* HUMPHRY, *knocks him to the ground.*

PETER. What did you say that for? What did you have to say that for?

HUMPHRY (*gets up, slightly shakily, smiles*). Because I've just been made a Senior Moral Tutor. It's our job to help people to see their little tangles more clearly.

PETER. But I've been a senior fucking moral what's-it for years, I don't go around insulting people and inviting them to hit me.

HUMPHRY. That's because you moved to Oxford. You've forgotten how seriously we take moral matters at Cambridge. I've got to be on my way if I'm going to just miss my train, and have an hour and a half hanging around Paddington waiting for the next. (*He goes to the door, turns.*) I suppose I'm sorry.

He exits.

There is a pause.

MARTIN. You all right?

PETER. Yes — yes — but I — I — why did he? That I should have hit Humpty, Of all people. Why did he?

MARTIN. I think — well, because he's so fond of you, isn't he? Fonder than of anyone else.

PETER. But I can't spend my life being what he needs me to be, can I?

MARTIN. No. You have to make your own life. I expect your being so prolific doesn't help either.

PETER. Yes well that's a different matter. He'd be ashamed to have written what I've written, but then he hasn't got a family — (*He stops.*) I've got to get to Hampstead. Christ, what a day, and the worst part hasn't even begun yet. You've realised what's happened, haven't you?

MARTIN. You've fallen in love with um, Jane, isn't it?

PETER (*nods*). It's a nightmare. Because what I said to Humpty was true. I love Sonia. I wouldn't hurt her for the world. Or the children — but Jane isn't just another — another of my fucks. I've got to get her out of my system.

MARTIN. I'm sorry about dinner tonight. If I could see any way —

PETER. No, I know. I had no right to involve you, really, had I? But you've been such a convenient fiction all these years. I must go or she will. And there's Roland — oh Christ!

STUART *whose steps have been sounding steadily, but not ostentatiously, through the above, enters.*

STUART. Oh hello. I didn't know you were coming down today.

PETER. Actually, I'm on my way. I've got to be in Hampstead — oh Christ, ten minutes ago, Martin will tell you all about it.

MARTIN. The chief thing is he's delivered his book.

STUART. Oh good.

PETER (*wryly*). Thanks. We'll sort out the various contractual problems in due course. Don't worry. I — I — (*He looks at them both.*) better go. Love to Marigold. (*He goes.*)

STUART (*crossing to desk*). What's been going on?

MARTIN. Oh, nothing really. He's fallen in love with somebody called Jane Papworth, wife of an Oxford theologian. And he has had the long-delayed climax with Humpty at last.

STUART. Humphry was here, was he? Pity. I'd like to have seen him. (*He sits down.*)

MARTIN. Michelle left early again, to read *Macbeth.*

STUART. Ah. And Marigold? Did she 'phone?

MARTIN. No, no news on the job.

STUART. Well, she said she'd come straight on here after the interview. So we'll hear, won't we?

MARTIN. Yes. You look tired. Did they give you a bad time?

STUART. Who?

MARTIN. The printers.

STUART. Actually, I didn't see them. Sorry.

MARTIN. Oh that's all right. Where did you go?

STUART. To the hospital.

MARTIN. Ah. How was he?

STUART. He's written eight new poems, especially for me. He still refuses to believe the magazine doesn't exist. He's been keeping the poems under his mattress. He thinks the nurses or doctors will try to steal them.

MARTIN. Any chance we could publish them? With an introduction by you. We might make a volume of it.

STUART. They're not eight new poems, they're eight shopping lists, on eight pieces of paper. A pound of apples, a calendar, a ball of wool, knitting needles, scissors, a — I forget what, oh, a turvey-drop.

MARTIN. What's a turvey-drop?

STUART. I don't know. The last order is for eight new poems in eight different rhyme schemes including one in terza rima, good to know he's still experimenting with verse form, isn't it, he's never written anything in terza rima before.

MARTIN. What did you do?

STUART. Oh, shuffled through the papers, nodding meaningfully, until he fell asleep. Or pretended to. His eyes were shut and he was snoring. But there was a funny little grin under his beard, like a snarl. When I got up to go he was clutching at my coat, it turned out. I had trouble prising myself free. I think he's terrified. And when you think of his best poems, they're mainly all about death. So urbane, so wise. Especially on his first wife. So seeing him like this is like a — a contamination.

MARTIN. Yes. Look, I know it sounds inadequate, but let's do something different tonight. Instead of going Greek, I'll book a table at where, L'Épicure. And if Marigold's interview —

STUART. Martin, I want to quit.

MARTIN. Quit?

STUART. Yes. Sorry. I didn't mean to blurt it out like that. I was wondering how to get around to it, as a matter of fact.

MARTIN. But why?

STUART. Because I'm no use to you.

MARTIN. Oh, don't be an idiot. Of course you are. For one thing, you're the poetry and fiction editor and —

STUART. Oh come on, we put out three novels a year, which we both really know are a sort of gift from you to me, especially as nobody but me likes them much, going by the speed at which they get remaindered at least. And as for poets, a few pamphlets which nobody reads, another gift from you to me, and Dougan and O'Leary, Leary and O'Dougan, whose shit is still exploding in our faces, though at least at a profit — which you deserve because you were bright enough to predict that they had a future as sort of middle-aged stars on the poetry pub circuit. I'm not blaming you for publishing them, you're absolutely right to, but the fact is I can't face reading them, let alone editing them, and that applies to every book we've got in the works at the moment, including probably especially Peter's latest.

MARTIN. But I was going to do Peter. And I don't mind doing Dougan and O'Leary either. In fact, I quite like them, not as poets I mean, I don't know about that — but for lunch and — (He gestures.) The point about them is that they're useful. And so is Peter. And when we've consolidated — in a year or so I worked it out this weekend — that's all, a year! — we'll have masses of work for you to do. On books you'll be proud to edit. Humpty's on Wagner, for instance. He virtually promised it to us this afternoon. In fact, I was going to ask you to go up to Cambridge and talk to him soon — I think he's a bit stuck with it, depressed. You could offer to read it for him — you're the only person whose judgement he really respects.

STUART. Of course I'll talk to him. And there's nothing I'd rather read than a book by Humphry on Wagner. Almost. But

I won't edit it. I have *got* to quit, Martin. You see, the real thing is — well, last night, just before you and Marigold got back from the concert, I was sitting in the kitchen drinking coffee and watching Martina strutting about on the counter. Then she did one of her things. You know, squatted on her haunches, arched her neck, stretched her legs. Went into a kind of trance of concentration. Aimed herself at the top of the fridge. And missed of course. No, she didn't. She caught the corner and ricochetted off, to the floor. And then she strutted away. Looking pleased with herself. And instead of finding her funny and endearing, I found myself thinking that either she was a freak — because a clumsy cat's a contradiction in terms, isn't it? Or she's a pervert. Because she *prefers* getting to the floor by way of a ricochet off the fridge. And I actually found myself loathing her as a — a — oh, obviously as a symbol of my — my — anyway, I went from loathing Martina to loathing it. My life I mean. And so back to first causes, and remembering that I only came in with you — well, you know why. To have children. Comfortably. You see. At your expense. I now realise. And there's quite a lot wrong with that on any terms, but especially if there aren't any children. To justify it. Partially.

MARTIN. But there will be. Why shouldn't there be? The tests showed you were both perfectly normal, you said, and Marigold's been pregnant once —

STUART. Yes, well that was obviously something of a miracle. So what we aborted might well have been the second coming. We're not going to have them. I know it in my bones. So does Marigold. (*He sits for a moment.*) Oh hell. How shameful that a literary gent like me can be ashamed of something that's not his fault. I lied over the tests, you see. What they showed was that I'm sterile. I produce a mere million or so sperms when only a hundred million or so will do. So it *was* a miracle, medically speaking. And it's not going to be repeated is it? Or it ceases to be a miracle. Which is what is required. (*He laughs slightly.*) The effect of this news has been to render me almost impotent as well. But that's likely to be only a passing phase. Once I stop being worried about being sterile, I'll probably become potent again. They tell me. All of which probably explains my loathing for Martina. Feeling at one with her, you see, a spayed freak. And that's why I've got to change something — my life here. The reason Marigold's so depressed, by the way, is that she blames herself more and more for killing off our only chance. You know what women are like — well, birth and the god's revenge, she's probably talked to you about it. And perhaps she's right. Anyway things aren't too good between us just now, as you've no doubt noticed. I know you have as you've been more than usually terrific even by your own high standards of delicacy and so forth. And having put almost all my cards on the table, I might as well plonk down the last one. *A propos* of dinner tonight, really. I really should quit for your sake too, you know. You shouldn't go on just being part of a trio, living for other people. You really need to be your own person at last. You do, Martin.

MARTIN *is about to speak, turns his head suddenly towards the door. The door opens.* MARIGOLD *enters.*

Hello darling, we were just wondering how the interview went. Or, in other words, did you get the job?

MARIGOLD. Not quite, I'm afraid.

MARTIN. Ah, well, in that case you'll probably need a drink.

STUART. I'll get it. I'm better at the preferred proportions, you tend to overdo the gin and underdo the tonic, Marigold recently confided to me. (*He goes to the drinks cabinet.*)

MARTIN *smiles at* MARIGOLD, *squeezes her hand comfortingly.*

But why not? Did they offer you any but the routine excuses, I mean having virtually insisted that you apply and having hinted heavily that it's as good as fixed — after all, you told them you weren't really sure you wanted it, even, I mean what the hell are they up to, in fact? (*Fixing a drink.*)

MARIGOLD. Oh, I suppose they decided that I wasn't Assistant Headmistress material.

STUART. What! (*He and* MARTIN *laugh*.)

MARIGOLD. No, that's not true. I might well be Assistant
Headmistress material for all I know, not knowing very much
but schools for the last ten years. But I didn't get the job
because I withdrew. No, I mean, I mean there was no
possibility of getting it because I withdrew. I didn't even go to
the interview.

STUART (*has stopped in front of her, holding her drink*). But
why not?

MARIGOLD. Because I didn't want it. May I? Thanks. (*She takes
the drink, takes a gulp*.) Sorry, but I do need it, as it turns out.
I don't know how to do this, though I've spent the day
working out different approaches. I determined to be simple.
And comprehensive. I'm pregnant you see. And have been for
some time. I've left it too late to choose, because I don't want
a choice. I'm going to have the baby, whatever. I think that's
all I worked out to say. (*She takes another gulp of her drink*.)
Sorry, chaps. (*She gives a little laugh*.)

STUART *looks at her, turns, looks at* MARTIN.

There is a pause.

STUART. Well, congratulations. (*Pause. He turns to*
MARIGOLD.) No, don't worry. You've managed the
traditional thing. Which is to tell the husband and father in
one breath, so to speak.

MARTIN. I suppose I'm sorry.

STUART. Though you're not.

MARTIN. Of course I'm not. How could I be? I've never wanted
anyone else in my life. From the moment I saw her. I've never
loved anyone else. Apart from you. So I'm sorry I hurt you,
is what I meant. Of all people. If it had been yours I'd have
loved it. But as it's mine, ours — (*He looks at* MARIGOLD.)

STUART. Well, I haven't got your capacity for decency, loyalty
etc. As it's yours I want to kill it. And you. And you. As a
matter of fact. I'll probably get over that in a few seconds.
And then we'll have what is called a talk. But I've no

intention of letting you go. (*To* MARIGOLD.) I love you too much. And we've spent far too many years — (*He looks at* MARTIN, *murderously. He goes and sits down, attempting to bring himself under control.*)

MARTIN. You should have told me. Let me deal with it. (*To* MARIGOLD.)

MARIGOLD. That wouldn't have been fair.

MARTIN. Yes. Well, I'm not letting you go either. How do we proceed?

STUART. I'll tell you how we proceed! (*He gets up.*)

There is the sound of feet on the stairs. Explosive coughing. Further coughing off, then the door opens.

NICK (*enters. He is smoking an enormous cigar. He coughs again*). This is a mistake. My agent gets them free on Concorde, she dishes them out as school prizes when we've done well. So you'll gather that the answer is yes, I am about to be a television star. You shall have the first kiss from a celebrity-soon, (*He kisses* MARIGOLD.) being my all time favourite lady and my first real love, I your chevalier. Before I break the bad news. Nappies has got the job too. We're going to be co-bloody presenting. Can you believe it! Apparently the Boring Buggers Corporation thinks Nappies and I complement each other, my brio striking off his lumpishness, I assume, so it'll be over to Nappies for Angus, back to me for Kingsley sort of stuff, but once they go over to me they won't be going over to him very often, I'll see to that, in fact I intend to make this my chance to wipe Nappies out of public life and back to wanking poesy, where he belongs, and I'll tell you something else, his agent told my agent — (*He stops.*) Is something the matter? A death been announced, or something? (*Looking around.*)

MARTIN. Nick, do you think you could go?

NICK. You want me to go?

STUART. Yes, Nick, please.

NICK (*after a pause*). Right. Well — (*He exits.*)

The sound of NICK *going downstairs, coughing. A door slams.*
Silence.

MARTIN (*to* STUART). Well?

The telephone on STUART's *desk rings.*

STUART (*lets it ring, then answers it*). Yes. Oh, hello. I see. Yes,
I will. No, no, don't worry, I'll tell him. Right. Well — I'm in
the middle of an important meeting right now, with one of
our authors, you see. Right. See you soon, I trust. 'Bye. (*He*
puts the telephone down. Pause.) That was Sonia. Her babysitter's let her down, she's still in Oxford, so she won't be able
to make dinner after all, she's sorry if she's caused any
problems.

MARTIN. Oh. (*Little pause.*) Right. (*Pause.*)

Lights.

Scene Two

MARTIN's *office. A few years later. Late Autumn. About 6.30 in*
the evening. Thin sunshine through the windows. The office door
is open. MARTIN's *jacket is over the back of his desk chair.*
STUART's *old desk is still there, but at a different angle, no*
longer directly facing MARTIN's.
      There is a bottle of whisky on MARTIN's *desk, and a glass*
with some whisky in it.
      NICK *is in the arm-chair, a drink in his hand. He is pale and*
gaunt.
      PETER *is lolling in the sofa, a drink in his hand.*

NICK (*after a pause*). What about 'Fear no more — '

PETER. Fear no more what?

NICK. The heat of the sun / Nor the furious winter's rages, /
Thou thy worldly task hast done / Home art gone and ta'en
thy wages / Golden lads and girls all must / As chimney

sweepers, come to — (*He wheezes uncontrollably, starts to cough violently. Sits breathing heavily, clearly shaken.*)

PETER. I thought you'd been ordered to stop.

NICK (*faintly*). Yes.

PETER. Emphysema, and you chain smoke.

NICK. Well, I still hold to my life's single principle. You don't live longer, it just seems — (*He coughs again rackingly.*)

The sound of footsteps, coming up the stairs.

PETER. But you'll never know, will you, how long it might have been. If you go on like this.

NICK. No. That's an extra perk.

MARTIN (*enters, in his shirt sleeves*). I know I heard footsteps. And there was an odd smell at the bottom of the stairs. Of alcohol and hospitals. Probably some old wino staggered in for a moment.

PETER. Or the ghost of Hubert Parkin. Came on ahead.

MARTIN. Well, I've risked leaving the door on the latch — so if he still turns up. He probably didn't get the message on his answering machine. He might not even be back. What train (*To* PETER.) are you catching?

PETER. The seven-forty. Sonia's dumping my lot on us for the weekend. It's sheer malice, as she's got nothing to do but look after the kids, which is all she's ever been up to anyway. So what with Jane's lot, there are going to be seven kids and the baby, and so with all the catering, the bed-making, the quarrels over sleeping-bags etc, she expects me back on the seven-forty. Can't say I blame her, poor love.

NICK. I was just saying, what about 'Fear no more'?

MARTIN. What?

PETER. The dirge. From *Cymbeline*. Nick's idea is to recite the first few lines, and then cough himself to death, he's got emphysema. And then we could have a double funeral.

MARTIN. Emphysema. (*He looks at* NICK.)

PETER. He's losing his lungs, day by day, inch by inch. And every cigarette he smokes —

MARTIN. You're an idiot, Nick.

PETER. How do you manage your cough on your dreadful programme? Or is that when they cut to Nappies, I've noticed his appearances have been getting longer.

NICK. Actually, Nappies is leaving. He's going to be theatre critic on the *Sunday Times,* apparently they're impressed by his lack of qualifications. But he's under the impression I'll allow him back now and then as my guest, to read out some of his wankings. We're having dinner (*He looks at his watch.*) to celebrate. Five minutes ago.

MARTIN. Nappies is coming over to me, did I tell you? We're publishing his next collection of poems.

NICK. Really, well he's not a bad poet, a bit derivative, but that's what he should stick to. As a matter of fact I'll miss him. One needs someone one hates meshed into the texture of one's life.

PETER. Look, we're not really getting anywhere, and we haven't much time.

The sound of footsteps on the stairs.

NICK. The thing is to be personal, dignified, simple and — (*He coughs, looks toward the door.*)

STUART *enters.*

STUART. Sorry. I only got in an hour ago. And your message came at the very end, and was cut off. The tape ran out I think. So all I really grasped was that you'd be here for a bit, but not for long.

There is a pause.

MARTIN. You got the bit about Humphry, did you?

STUART. Only that he was dead. (*He sits down.*) Was it suicide?

PETER. Sort of.

MARTIN. Though in fact he was murdered. Somebody he picked

up in the Cambridge market-place. At the tea-stall actually. Humpty took him back and — (*He gestures.*)

NICK. Apparently he didn't put up much of a fight. Just let himself be beaten to death.

MARTIN. He was naked, apparently.

PETER. Except for a sock.

MARTIN. We'd heard what he was getting up to. The risks he was taking. I think we all tried to warn him.

STUART. Yes, I did too. We had lunch just before I left.

MARTIN. Have a drink?

STUART. Thanks.

He gets a glass. MARTIN *pours him a drink.*

STUART. Thanks.

PETER. He anticipated it. For one thing he left some stuff in an envelope. A letter to me. Which I won't go into because it was characteristically scathing.

MARTIN. And some poems. About a dozen. With a note saying that they were for you. He'd started writing poetry again about six months before. But the reason we're meeting is that his father is in a state of shock. The mother died last year and he's, what, nearly eighty. Anyway he asked me to organise the funeral. He wants to do the right thing you see. And he wants to have something characteristic of Humphry, whom he obviously didn't know very well. We've pretty well got to decide tonight. I have to 'phone Trinity tomorrow, and let the Master know what we've proposed. He hopes it won't be anything too bizarre, as he'll be there himself, of course.

PETER. I should think so. For one of their Senior Moral Tutors.

MARTIN. So far we've had proposals of a brief reading of those poems he wouldn't let you publish when he was an undergraduate — I know you've always kept copies. And the new poems, if you think they're appropriate. And the introduction to the Wagner book he never wrote.

NICK. And 'Fear no more'. (*He coughs badly.*)

STUART. I thought you'd given up.

NICK *sits wheezing, gestures.*

I can't see that that's appropriate. Golden lads and girls all must — Humphry was scarcely a golden lad. And thou thy worldly task hast done — what partly killed him was that he couldn't perform his worldly task. At least to his standards. And as for Wagner and having his own poems read, well — he'd have viewed it with his usual contempt.

PETER. Well then what? He always respected you most. You decide. (*He glances at his watch.*)

STUART. I'd have thought the traditional Church of England service, in the traditional version. He'd have wanted to please his father, wouldn't he, he always took such care of him.

A pause.

MARTIN. I agree.

NICK *coughs, nods.*

PETER. Sure.

MARTIN. And one of us can make a short and telling speech. In the Humpty style, but sweeter, naturally. (*To* STUART.) Will you do it?

STUART. Of course. But actually, from Humpty's point of view, I think Peter should. As he's the one of us Humpty loved. Most, anyway.

PETER. Yes, I had an idea it would come out like that. All right.

NICK (*getting up*). So that's settled then? I mustn't keep Nappies waiting more than half an hour, he might take offence and stay on the programme. Oh, Stuart, have you seen that stuff from your agent yet? About appearing for us. Me.

STUART. Well, I only glanced at it. But thanks Nick. I'd like to.

NICK. We'll get together. But the thing is to keep it anecdotal. Your own experience of Parkin, that sort of thing. People still don't know much about his poems. But we'll plug the book, don't worry.

STUART. Thanks.

PETER (*to* NICK, *who has also got up*). I'll come with you. You can drop me. It's a good book, Stuart. I wish I could write something like it. You didn't care for him very much, did you?

STUART. Not as much as I hoped when I began. Congratulations on Leeds, by the way. I meant to write you a note.

PETER. It's a dump with a chair in it. The only one I'll ever be offered, so I've got no choice. Jane sends her love by the way. Next time you're in Oxford — or Leeds, from next term —

NICK. Peter, if you're coming —

PETER. Right.

NICK *and* PETER *go*.

There is a pause.

MARTIN. So how was New York?

STUART. OK. A lot of lectures, interviews, all that. Like Nick, they're not much interested in Parkin's poetry. Only his life. Especially in its brutal beginning and its spectacular degeneration.

MARTIN. Do you mind if we do a different cover? We're not keen on the American one. We'll show you some ideas — we've got a very bright girl.

STUART. Right.

MARTIN (*putting on his jacket*). Oh. Here's Humpty's stuff. (*Taking a packet out of his pocket, handing it to* STUART.) And if you think they should be published, perhaps you'd do the introduction?

STUART. Yes. If they're any good.

MARTIN. Right. Look, I've got to go. I'm meeting (*Slight hesitation.*) Marigold for dinner, our once-a-week outing. Our babysitter — Michelle, by the way, re-doing her 'A' levels full time — doesn't allow us out late. So if you want to stay and have a drink — and lock up after. You don't need a key — but you know the procedure. I haven't made copies of the poems yet, you see, so we'd better not risk —

STUART. No, right. I'll look at them here. How is Marigold?

MARTIN. She's fine.

STUART. And the twins.

MARTIN. They're fine.

STUART. Good. And Martina?

MARTIN. Martina? Oh! I'm afraid we had to have her put down.
All mine as well. Including Samantha. The twins are asthmatic,
you see, and the cats were too old to find a new home for.
We'd have offered you Martina back, of course, but you're
away so much these days —

STUART *nods.*

MARTIN. We're moving out of here. We're looking for premises
on two floors.

STUART. I'm sure that's the right thing to do.

MARTIN. Might you come and see Marigold and the twins one
day? She'd like that.

STUART. Oh, one day I'm sure I will.

They look at each other. MARTIN *smiles.* STUART *smiles
back.*

MARTIN *goes to his glass, picks it up, holds it out to* STUART.

MARTIN. Humpty, eh?

STUART. Yes. Humpty. (*He lifts his glass.*)

MARTIN (*little pause*). Do you think Humpty was the best of us?
I've been wondering that since it happened.

STUART. Well, he didn't mess up any lives except his own. I
suppose. Except — I suppose the wretched creature he
probably provoked into murdering him. Have they caught
him?

MARTIN. Oh yes. Trying to flog his hi-fi and a whole stack of
records. He didn't give himself a chance. (*He drains off the
glass.*) Well then, if not the best, then the first to go. If Nick

doesn't look out he'll be next.

STUART. That doesn't follow. What you mean is that he deserves to be next.

MARTIN (*laughs*). Yes. Stuart — (*He stops.*) Please come and see us. She misses you dreadfully, of course.

He turns and goes out quickly.

STUART *sits for a moment, then gets up, goes to* MARTIN's *desk, looks at it then crosses to his old desk. He turns on the desk light, sits down, takes the poems out of the envelope. He begins to read, as:*

Strains of Wagner, in full and majestic flow, towards the end side of the record from Act One, Scene One.

STUART *takes his spectacles out of his pocket, puts them on, settles to read as Wagner continues. He remains in this position as the set revolves off, while the Cambridge room revolves on, the music coming from the gramophone, for the Epilogue.*

Epilogue

STUART's *rooms in Cambridge. Twenty years ago and about fifteen minutes on from Act One, Scene One. Wagner is in full and majestic flow.* MARTIN *is still in his intensely-listening posture.* PETER *is sitting, casually, looking through a pocket diary.* HUMPHRY *is watching* NICK, *who is standing in the centre of the room, conducting and humming along with Wagner.*

HUMPHRY, *not noticed by* NICK, *gets up, goes over, turns off the record in mid-bar.*

NICK *hums and conducts a second longer. He stops.*

HUMPHRY *puts the record away.*

NICK. I was just getting into it, what did you do that for?

HUMPHRY. Because I don't enjoy having Wagner trivialised.

NICK. But I'm deeply fond of Wagner. (*To* PETER.) Aren't I?

PETER (*laughs*). Yes, you are, quite.

HUMPHRY (*looks at* PETER, *then to* NICK). I wasn't talking about you, I was talking about the performance. In fact, your conducting was probably marginally better than the conductor's.

NICK. Thank you. (*He bows, as if on a podium.*)

STUART *and* MARIGOLD *enter,* STUART *in a state of controlled excitement.*

STUART. Oh, hello everybody, I'm very sorry.

MARIGOLD. Yes.

PETER. Where have you been?

STUART. Talking to Hubert Parkin.

NICK. Hubert Parkin!

STUART. Yes, the thing is we saw him crossing the court to one of the guest rooms, he was at the feast last night. So I nobbled him.

NICK. You mean to say that while we've been seething passionately away in here, close to violence from time to time, you two have been calmly having it off with Hubert Parkin! And you didn't come and tell us!

STUART. I wanted to talk to him about the magazine. He was very interested. He might even contribute a poem.

MARIGOLD. Actually, he virtually promised.

STUART. Although it'll depend on what our first issue looks like, I imagine. The point is that meeting him today seemed like a sort of omen. Anyway, let's get started. Oh, Marigold, this is Humphry Taylor, who sent in the poems I told you about, Marigold Watson.

MARIGOLD. Hello.

STUART. And this is um, um, I'm terribly sorry.

MARTIN. Martin Musgrove.

STUART. Who's offered to take over the advertising, business etc.

MARTIN. All the really boring stuff, in fact, is my level. (*To* MARIGOLD, *smiles.*)

STUART. Well then, um — let's —

HUMPHRY. As a matter of fact, I just wanted to pick up my poems.

STUART. Why?

HUMPHRY. I'm not really happy with them. You see —

STUART. Well, there's lots of time for revisions. They're not into proof yet, after all. (*Little laugh.*) I mean — you still want to be associated with the magazine, don't you? (*In sudden alarm.*) All we want to talk about is what we think it should stand for. Whether we should issue a manifesto. What should be in it. And the financial stuff, of course.

HUMPHRY *makes to speak.*

Although I'll be titular editor, as the founding father, so to speak, and anyway somebody has to be, but I want us to be a nucleus. A creative nucleus. Feeding off each other.

NICK. Yes, but is there going to be a theatre column?

STUART. Come on, Nick. We'll get to that in due course. Let's begin by being absolutely clear about what we want to happen. What it is precisely we want to offer the world.

NICK *goes into a coughing spasm, which he turns into a theatrical event, culminating in a collapse backwards into a chair.*

NICK. Whoops! Sorry. If this goes on, I'm going to have to think seriously about taking up another sort of cigarette. Or replacing smoking with sex. Hey, if we don't have a theatre page, can we have a sex page? Marigold and I can do it together can't we Marigold? Or Peter and Sonia? If I choose to bring them together. *And* Marigold and I? Well?

STUART *and* MARIGOLD *laugh.*
HUMPHRY *lets out a little laugh.*

MARIGOLD. Shut up, Nick.

MARTIN *grins.*

STUART. Yes, shut up Nick. Now where were we?

A slight pause.

MARTIN. Um. What were we about to give the world. Wasn't it?

Lights.

Curtain.

Methuen's Modern Plays

Jean Anouilh	*Antigone*
	Becket
	The Lark
John Arden	*Serjeant Musgrave's Dance*
	The Workhouse Donkey
	Armstrong's Last Goodnight
John Arden and	*The Business of Good Government*
Margaretta D'Arcy	*The Royal Pardon*
	The Hero Rises Up
	The Island of the Mighty
	Vandaleur's Folly
Wolfgang Bauer	*Shakespeare the Sadist*
Rainer Werner	
Fassbinder	*Bremen Coffee*
Peter Handke	*My Foot My Tutor*
Frank Xaver Kroetz	*Stallerhof*
Brendan Behan	*The Quare Fellow*
	The Hostage
	Richard's Cork Leg
Edward Bond	*A-A-America!* and *Stone*
	Saved
	Narrow Road to the Deep North
	The Pope's Wedding
	Lear
	The Sea
	Bingo
	The Fool and *We Come to the River*
	Theatre Poems and Songs
	The Bundle
	The Woman
	The Worlds with *The Activists Papers*
	Restoration and *The Cat*
	Summer and *Fables*
Bertolt Brecht	*Mother Courage and Her Children*
	The Caucasian Chalk Circle
	The Good Person of Szechwan
	The Life of Galileo

The Threepenny Opera
Saint Joan of the Stockyards
The Resistible Rise of Arturo Ui
The Mother
Mr Puntila and His Man Matti
The Measures Taken and other Lebrstücke
The Days of the Commune
The Messingkauf Dialogues
Man Equals Man and *The Elephant Calf*
The Rise and Fall of the City of Mahagonny and *The Seven Deadly sins*
Baal
A Respectable Wedding and other one-act plays
Drums in the Night
In the Jungle of Cities
Fear and Misery of the Third Reich and *Senora Carrar's Rifles*

Brecht ⎫
Weill   ⎬   *Happy End*
Lane   ⎭
Howard Brenton   *The Churchill Play*
                 Weapons of Happiness
                 Epsom Downs
                 The Romans in Britain
                 Plays for the Poor Theatre
                 Magnificence
                 Revenge
                 Hitler Dances

Howard Brenton and
David Hare   *Brassneck*
Mikhail Bulgakov *The White Guard*
Noël Coward   *Hay Fever*
Shelagh Delaney *A Taste of Honey*
                 The Lion in Love
David Edgar   *Destiny*
                 Mary Barnes

Michael Frayn	*Clouds*
	Alphabetical Order and Donkey's Years
	Make and Break
	Noises Off
	Benefactors
Max Frisch	*The Fire Raisers*
	Andorra
	Triptych
Jean Giraudoux	*The Trojan War Will Not Take Place*
Simon Gray	*Butley*
	Otherwise Engaged and other plays
	Dog Days
	The Rear Column and other plays
	Close of Play and Pig in a Poke
	Stage Struck
	Quartermaine's Terms
Peter Handke	*Offending the Audience* and *Self-Accusation*
	Kaspar
	The Ride Across Lake Constance
Kaufman & Hart	*They Are Dying Out*
	Once in a Lifetime, You Can't Take It With You and *The Man Who Came To Dinner*
Barrie Keeffe	*Gimme Shelter (Gem, Gotcha, Getaway)*
	Barbarians (Killing Time, Abide With Me, In the City)
	A Mad World, My Masters
Arthur Kopit	*Indians*
	Wings
John McGrath	*The Cheviot, the Stag and the Black, Black Oil*
David Mamet	*Glengarry Glen Ross*
David Mercer	*After Haggerty*
	The Bankrupt and other plays
	Cousin Vladimir and *Shooting the Chandelier*
	Duck Song
	Huggy Bear and other plays

	The Monster of Karlovy Vary and *Then and Now*
	No Limits To Love
Arthur Miller	*The American Clock*
Percy Mtwa, Mbongeni Ngema, Barney Simon	*Woza Albert*
Peter Nichols	*Passion Play*
	Poppy
Joe Orton	*Loot*
	What the Butler Saw
	Funeral Games and *The Good and Faithful Servant*
	Entertaining Mr Sloane
	Up Against It
Harold Pinter	*The Birthday Party*
	The Room and *The Dumb Waiter*
	The Caretaker
	A Slight Ache and other plays
	The Collection and *The Lover*
	The Homecoming
	Tea Party and other plays
	Landscape and *Silence*
	Old Times
	No Man's Land
	Betrayal
	The Hothouse
	Other Places (A Kind of Alaska, Victoria Station, Family Voices)
Luigi Pirandello	*Henry IV*
	Six Characters in Search of an Author
Stephen Poliakoff	*Hitting Town* and *City Sugar*
David Rudkin	*The Sons of Light*
	The Triumph of Death
Jean-Paul Sartre	*Crime Passionnel*
Wole Soyinka	*Madmen and Specialists*
	The Jero Plays
	Death and the King's Horseman
C.P. Taylor	*And a Nightingale Sang . . .*

	Good
Peter Whelan	*The Accrington Pals*
Nigel Williams	*Line 'Em*
	Class Enemy
Charles Wood	*Veterans*
Theatre Workshop	*Oh What a Lovely War!*
Various authors	*Best Radio Plays of 1978* (Don Haworth: *Episode on a Thursday Evening:* Tom Mallin: *Halt! Who Goes There?*; Jennifer Phillips: *Daughters of Men;* Fay Weldon: *Polaris;* Jill Hyem: *Remember Me;* Richard Harris: *Is It Something I Said?*)
	Best Radio Plays of 1979 (Shirley Gee: *Typhoid Mary;* Carey Harrison: *I Never Killed My German;* Barrie Keeffe: *Heaven Scent;* John Kirkmorris: *Coxcombe;* John Peacock: *Attard in Retirement;* Olwen Wymark: *The Child*)
	Best Radio Plays of 1982 (Rhys Adrian:*Watching the Plays Together;* John Arden: *The Old Man Sleeps Alone;* Harry Barton: *Hoopoe Day;* Donald Chapman: *Invisible Writing;* Tom Stoppard: *The Dog It Was That Died;* William Trevor: *Autumn Sunshine*)

The Master Playwrights

Collections of plays by the best-known modern playwrights in value-for-money paperbacks.

John Arden **PLAYS: ONE**
Serjeant Musgrave's Dance, The Workhouse Donkey, Armstrong's Last Goodnight

Brendan Behan **THE COMPLETE PLAYS**
The Hostage, The Quare Fellow, Richard's Cork Leg, Moving Out, A Garden Party, The Big House

Edward Bond **PLAYS: ONE**
Saved, Early Morning, The Pope's Wedding
PLAYS: TWO
Lear, The Sea, Narrow Road to the Deep North, Black Mass, Passion

Noël Coward **PLAYS: ONE**
Hay Fever, The Vortex, Fallen Angels, Easy Virtue
PLAYS: TWO
Private Lives, Bitter Sweet, The Marquise, Post-Mortem
PLAYS: THREE
Design for Living, Cavalcade, Conversation Piece, and *Hands Across the Sea, Still Life* and *Fumed Oak* from *Tonight at 8.30*
PLAYS: FOUR
Blithe Spirit, This Happy Breed, Present Laughter and *Ways and Means, The Astonished Heart* and *Red Peppers* from *Tonight at 8.30*
PLAYS: FIVE
Relative Values, Look After Lulu, Waiting in the Wings, Suite in Three Keys

John Galsworthy **FIVE PLAYS**
Strife, The Eldest Son, The Skin Game, Justice, Loyalties

Henrik Ibsen	*Translated and introduced by Michael Meyer* PLAYS: ONE *Ghosts, The Wild Duck, The Master Builder* PLAYS: TWO *A Doll's House, An Enemy of the People,* *Hedda Gabler* *PLAYS: THREE* *Rosmersholm, Little Eyolf, The Lady from* *the Sea* PLAYS: FOUR *John Gabriel Borkman, The Pillars of Society,* *When We Dead Awaken*
Molière	FIVE PLAYS *The Misanthrope, Tartuffe, The School for* *Wives, The Miser, The Hypochondriac*
Clifford Odets	SIX PLAYS *Waiting for Lefty, Awake and Sing! Till the* *Day I Die, Paradise Lost, Golden Boy,* *Rocket to the Moon (introduced by Harold* *Clurman)*
Joe Orton	THE COMPLETE PLAYS *Entertaining Mr Sloane, Loot, What the* *Butler Saw, The Ruffian on the Stair, The* *Erpingham Camp, Funeral Games, The* *Good and Faithful Servant*
Harold Pinter	PLAYS: ONE *The Birthday Party, The Room, The Dumb* *Waiter, A Slight Ache, A Night Out* PLAYS: TWO *The Caretaker, Night School, The Dwarfs,* *The Collection, The Lover, five revue* *sketches* PLAYS: THREE *The Homecoming, Tea Party, The Basement,* *Landscape, Silence, six revue sketches* PLAYS: FOUR *Old Times, No Man's Land, Betrayal,* *Monologue, Family Voices*

Terrence Rattigan	PLAYS: ONE *French Without Tears, The Winslow Boy,* *The Browning Version, Harlequinade*
Strindberg	*Introduced and translated by Michael Meyer* PLAYS: ONE *The Father, Miss Julie, The Ghost Sonata* PLAYS: TWO *The Dance of Death, A Dream Play, The* *Stronger*
J.M. Synge	THE COMPLETE PLAYS *In the Shadow of the Glen, Riders to the* *Sea, The Tinker's Wedding. The Well of the* *Saints, The Playboy of the Western World,* *Deirdre of the Sorrows*
Oscar Wilde	THREE PLAYS *Lady Windermere's Fan, An Ideal Husband,* *The Importance of Being Earnest*
P.G. Wodehouse	FOUR PLAYS *The Play's the Thing, Good Morning, Bill,* *Leave it to Psmith, Come On, Jeeves*

Methuen's Theatre Classics

Büchner   DANTON'S DEATH
                 (English version by Howard Brenton)
                 WOYZECK
                 (translated by John MacKendrick; introduced
                 by Michael Patterson)
Chekhov   THE CHERRY ORCHARD
                 THREE SISTERS
                 (translated and introduced by Michael Frayn)
                 UNCLE VANYA
                 (English version by Pam Gems; introduced by
                 Edward Braun)
                 WILD HONEY
                 (translated, adapted and introduced by Michael
                 Frayn)
Euripides   THE BACCHAE
                 (English version by Wole Soyinka)
Gogol   THE GOVERNMENT INSPECTOR
                 (translated by Edward O. Marsh and Jeremy
                 Brooks; introduced by Edward Braun)
Gorky   ENEMIES
                 THE LOWER DEPTHS
                 (translated by Kitty Hunter-Blair and Jeremy
                 Brooks; introduced by Edward Braun)
Granville Barker THE MADRAS HOUSE
                 (introduced by Margery Morgan)
Hauptmann   THE WEAVERS
                 (translated and introduced by Frank Marcus)
Ibsen   BRAND
                 GHOSTS
                 PEER GYNT
                 (translated and introduced by Michael Meyer)
Jarry   THE UBU PLAYS
                 (translated by Cyril Connolly and Simon
                 Watson-Taylor; edited with an introduction
                 by Simon Watson-Taylor)
Schnitzler   LA RONDE
                 (translated by Frank and Jacqueline Marcus)

ANATOL
(translated by Frank Marcus)

Synge THE PLAYBOY OF THE WESTERN
WORLD
(introduced by T.R. Henn)

Tolstoy THE FRUITS OF ENLIGHTENMENT
(translated and introduced by Michael Frayn)

Wedekind SPRING AWAKENING
*(translated by Edward Bond; introduced by
Edward and Elisabeth Bond)*

Wilde THE IMPORTANCE OF BEING
EARNEST
(introduced by Adeline Hartcup)
LADY WINDERMERE'S FAN
(introduced by Hesketh Pearson)